vision | romance | espresso | God | anci...

ENTER THE WORSHIP CIRCLE

aanbidden adorar tapmak
verehren adhuroj wiebie

BEN PASLEY

Enter The Worship Circle

Published by Relevant Books
A division of Relevant Media Group, Inc.

www.relevant-books.com
www.relevantmediagroup.com

© 2001 by Relevant Media Group, Inc.

Cover design by Boyd Dupree

Internal design by Relevant Solutions
Bobby Jones, Daniel Ariza
www.relevant-solutions.com

Library of Congress Catalog Number: 2001119645
International Standard Book Number: 088419-792-1

For information:

RELEVANT MEDIA GROUP, INC.
POST OFFICE BOX 951127
LAKE MARY, FL 32795
407-333-7152
info@relevantmediagroup.com

Confessions From The Author

I want to invite you into a mystical world.

Telling you now is important. If you know my intent, then you can better prepare for the experience. In the following pages I want to unfold some of the ongoing spiritual adventure that has changed my life, and, it is my belief, that this amazing adventure may lead to a life-changing experience for you as well.

Why believe that I have anything to offer?

Maybe I am a religion salesman. Maybe just a book salesman. I realize that I can't clearly prove my motive at this point, but I am willing to risk inviting you in to the journey because I believe you will prove for yourself if it is genuine. Everyone has a story of some kind, and some are compelled to share. My story is wrapped up in a life-changing interaction with God, and in the following pages I will share a little of it—the part that has to do with worship.

In the way of personal introduction, I will make some confessions.

I love to create. As a musician and songwriting performer I have traveled all over the States and to many places overseas weaving instruments and voices together. I enjoy the fusion of ethnic sounds and modern music, and I have recently become infatuated with combining creative expressions like dance, painting, and film into multi-art concerts. This book is a fusion experiment. I have combined narrative fiction, offbeat prose, personal essays, and mystical visions into a book that touches the supernatural. This fusion of voices, like improvisational music, is working to tell a single story, but it will take time. I have risked the experiment hoping you will stay with me until the final page is turned.

Bring your imagination and your experience to this improv.

Weave your own world into the margins of this book.

 I also confess that when I write songs, whether in the studio or spontaneously in concert, it is a revelation of the pictures in my head. This book is written from the same perspective. Some of the pictures I am going to relay have been part of my own life experience—my personal story. Some of them have come to me like visions or one-act plays from the edge of my imagination. Some of them fell from my fingers as I sat down to type like songs fall from the guitar when I sit down to play.

There are several pictures and seven voices in this book.

Each of these voices speak into the adventure of worship, God, eternity, and human experience from a different angle. Together they are like different people, each looking through different windows of the same building, as they tell us about what they see inside. Not all of them agree, but if taken together they will bring insight into what it means to "Enter the Worship Circle." I have placed "signs" throughout the adventure to help identify the separate voices—they appear like symbols over each scene or chapter and provide a quick reference for which voice is speaking.

So, if you are ready, let me invite you again into a mystical world. If my discoveries are true, then I pray this book will serve as a doorway for you to enter into the mystery of worship, interaction with God, and the unfolding adventure of eternity.

Some things are just too wonderful *not* to share.

Table Of Voices

Here we listen to the thoughts of an obsessive coffee lover who narrates his own journey into the separate worlds of espresso and worship. The two worlds intertwine over years of experience.

People from all walks of life, different points of history, and different religious backgrounds look into themselves, into worship, and into the texture of their experience. They speak to us about what they see.

The author speaks in open conversation. From the places in the mind where eternal things are considered and truth is searched out, these essays give voice to the questions and convictions of the writer.

A singular voice, an aspiring mountain climber, journals his experience to the achievement of a lifetime, leaving clues for those who would follow along the way.

A Seeker of Truth is taken up into a vision so powerful, so clear, that we are able to see through her eyes and hear through her ears into the world beyond—the world of the supernatural.

The creative arts are given a voice to speak. They reveal the tensions of their birth, their role in connecting humanity with the eternal, and their passion to be involved in worship.

An encourager places a collection of seven challenges at different points along the journey—each collection opening up a new experience in worship.

Java

Wandering into the coffee shop was a rescue from my lonely apartment. Sure, I could make some average coffee at my place and drink it with my own set of coffeehouse-like gear, but then I would be alone, and I would be consigned to share my caffeineated thoughts with the sheetrock walls and the messy kitchen. *It was good to be around people*, I thought, as I pressed into the dimly lit room. It was warm with the smell of the coffee roaster and the buzz of the machinery.

This was not my normal stop. Some of my friends kept saying, "What? You still go to that old place on the west side? You need to check out Café Mystique!" Well, I figured with a campy name like Café Mystique that some middle-aged wife of a successful businessman had opened up the shop in hopes of reconnecting with her hippie years. Even if it were true, she was nowhere in sight, and behind the counter a couple of young beatniks were making java drinks. I could tell from the way they worked that they were definitely in touch with their inner barista.

Weaving past the entry tables and some heavy furniture, I made my way to the counter. Since it was my first time there I had to give it my "Virgin Coffeehouse Test." I would order the double Macchiato, I would *not* look at the menu, and I would make sure they knew that I was not looking at the menu. Several things at stake here. If they had to ask me what a "Macchiato" was then the game would be over and I would order something else because they didn't deserve to make it.

They did not ask—great so far.

Then I waited to see if they would confuse me with the average Starbucks patron (with a limited Starbucks menu vocabulary) and make me one of those oversized milk-meets-syrup beverages with the swirls on top.

It didn't happen—joy.

Next were the presentation issues: Would the cup be warmed before the espresso shot? Would they center the dry milk foam into the espresso cream so that the tan layer would fold up around the edges? Wooden stick or tiny spoon?

Before I had time to fill in the rest of their "Virgin" score card I noticed that the far wall was covered with an unusual art collection. It was some kind of neo-caveman collection that stuck out from the wall and just begged for attention. There was textured stuff like wood, rough clay, and grass weavings. These ancient things were combined with what looked like the guts to computers, machinery, and high-tech bombs. It conjured up visions of a mad inventor cackling and hammering away in his loincloth, MIT degree on the wall behind him, fully committed to using both an ax and a soldering iron. My eyes were adjusted to the room now and I could see phrases plastered across the front of each art piece. I could just barely read one of them.

"Sir...excuse me...dollar-seventy-nine?" came the voice across the counter.

I had the change, I took my drink, and I headed back to get a little closer to the art piece that housed this phrase:

Worship

In Fire

I see a pile of stones neatly stacked together here on top of the hill. In every direction I can see the horizon around me, except to the north where the grove of trees has raised its branches to block my view. The ashes from recent offerings smolder in and around the pit. "Sum dee li ay onphay koh, sum dee li ay onphay koh…" is the chanted song that always accompanies the familiar smells of the sacred area.

When I first step into the circle of rocks I remember my mother. When I was a little boy my mother would sing the lines in a hushed voice over me and around the house late in the evening when we were put to bed. The same words fill my mouth, and I half-speak, half-sing them in the same hushed voice as I walk, stepping carefully over and around some other worshipers, toward the center where the sacred pole rises from the ground. Inscribed with pictures that tell the story, the pole is blackened on one side from the altar fires, but I can still see the sign of the sun, part of the story of the war, and the eye of god. The eye always follows me when I walk.

The bearded man who cares for the sacred place all day looks as if he slept in the ashes all night. His small, blackened hands take my offering. His eyes, red from the smoke, look at my offering, look through me, and quickly turn back to the altar where he performs his duties; kneeling, I perform mine. Soon the smoke from my burning offering and the chants of the gathering will rise together into the sky over the sacred hill.

The crops were bad this year. All of my people suffered from the curse of the poor harvest and the sickness that came with the hunger. One of my children was terribly ill. As my offering burns slowly to black on the altar I pray that we will be helped. I pray that we will be forgiven. I pray that we will not be punished any longer. Maybe the eye that follows me will also see the desperation in my heart and find some mercy to share.

I feel small, helpless, but very glad that I have come to worship fire today.

The Alarm Clock Moment

In our world we no longer admire teachers as much as we admire helpers. Teachers, in our mind, come with a pre-packaged lesson plan and give lectures that we should write down. Helpers, on the other hand, come to us with personal concern and a belief that we have inside of us the tools to excel, but we simply need encouragement and maybe a working model to follow. For the academic mind this rings of "inductive versus deductive" theories of learning—the difference between discovering through experience and flatly assuming the points of a lecture. Being "taught" implies that we don't already know something, but being "helped" supports our position that we have all we need—we simply need a little encouragement to help us find it.

This short journey into the Worship Circle may offer some help in reaching our ultimate destination. Just what is that destination? We know that it is not found in the material world. "Things" do not contain the kind of treasure that we seek. We all seem to be searching for something genuinely trustworthy in life, and we all have a sense that this search has something to do with the mystery of eternity and the world beyond. This common pursuit leads us to the common need for a *helper*—someone or something that can challenge us to discover Truth. No one has to teach us that we should hunger for the supernatural; the hunger is already in us—and we know it.

No one can hand it to us.

My suspicion is that we all have a capacity to become great, to do well, and to move to the next level of living, but we often miss our opportunity to "wake up" to the best kind of motivation. Many people stay up late waiting for the "late-night-infomercial-you-didn't-know-you-needed-this-did-you?" kind of motivation that dissipates after coffee the next morning. This kind of motivation is external and temporary. The motivation that we need to excel must come from deep within.

Humanity possesses a myriad of these deep, internal motivations: some physical, some mental, and some supernatural. To deny any one of these motivators' proper exercise is to deny one's own human essence. Humans are driven to use their physical capacities to move, communicate, and express themselves. Humans must exercise the ability to think, dream, and engage the world with their minds. And, without a doubt, humans are obsessed with discovering a meaningful interaction with the world beyond its fingertips in order to exercise the spiritual part of life.

The question for us is: Have we given proper exercise to each of these areas?

In the physical realm we are constantly coached and challenged to work our way into better condition. Be thinner, taller, tighter, and sexier! Fitness and physical beauty is a mega-million dollar industry. The free-market is well aware that we are easily motivated to improve our body and "look." The challenge to improve ourselves physically might often come from *without*, but it gains momentum when fueled by the ready passion from *within*. No one has to teach us to celebrate the winner of the decathlon or to admire the beauty of the human form. The real challenge is not in deciding to improve physically, but the decision *how* it will be done.

Concerning the mental realm, it might be fun to pick on the "brain" of the class in the sixth grade, but by the time we graduate from college we see things in a different light. That same "brain" is now driving the car we want and making the money we wish we had. The passage of time proves that being smart…is smart. Movies, books, and history are filled with the stories of the thinkers, writers, and solution people who changed the world. Communities spend millions of dollars on education and mental training to advance the thinking part of the individual because it will boost the subsequent wealth of the community. In this new global economy we all strive to think smarter, read faster, outwit our adversary, and recover quickly from the personal computer crash. It is now a brain-sport world, and we are all searching for the path to excellence.

Throughout history the supernatural part of man has been just as challenged as the physical and mental parts, because it is just as real and ready for inspiration. Recently, however, we have entered a new era of intense spiritual pursuit. Something has happened in our world community that has shifted us into mystical overdrive. Now our challenge is not *whether we will* exercise our internal drive to reach out to the supernatural, it is *how we will reach out*. The new confusion is that in our modern world of computers, television, and cars we have access to all the external voices—and they are all competing for supremacy. We are challenged to get in touch with our spirit guides via 900 numbers, we can find our cosmic center through the huge New Age section at the bookstore, and we can watch The *X-Files* almost any day of the week. We can get *Touched by an Angel*, or freak watching The *Blair Witch Project*, or entertain ourselves with any number of apocalyptic myths that the new millennium has ushered in. For a more heady approach we are pressed to read Hume, Nietzsche, C.S. Lewis, and Asimov for religious or irreligious views on religion. In-a-"pinch" prayer is always good—even for the athiest—and many of us are experimenting with churches and religious gatherings with either ourselves or our children in mind. We have come to grips with the fact that we have supernatural urges—deep internal motivation—but where do we go from here? How do we properly exercise this desire?

No one can hand it to us.

While some might try to capitalize on this spiritual awakening in pursuit of our bank accounts, there must be some who are willing to give us a compass, an encouragement, and a gesture toward the horizon without ulterior motive. There must be some "helpers" out there who want to see the look on our collective face as we discover for ourselves what is real and exciting about the supernatural world. We are all on a spiritual mountain climb, and this book is designed to *help*.

To enter the Worship Circle is to enter the world of the supernatural with a freedom to experiment, to discover its treasures, and to find its center—the goal of our mystical pursuit. Worship, itself, will help us embrace the surest part of the world beyond and mature in our experience with it. Worship will exercise our supernatural life. Without exercise this spiritual life would atrophy and fade away leaving us less whole, less alive, and *less human*. This adventure into the Worship Circle can help us to not only "wake up" what may have fallen asleep, but also to make decisions about our spiritual path among all the competing voices.

No one can hand it to us.

Will we reach out to find it?

Java Boy **Xpresso**

Everything that touched the floor of the coffeehouse was from the style era known as Early University Eclectic. Chairs that had no twin in the room hemmed in hand-painted tables, and a couch sat recently recovered in dark purple velvet. *Thank God*, I mused, looking toward the ceiling—somebody had the courage to spend a lot of money on the lighting. Funky little table lamps provided some warm glow around the corners and nooks, and overhead were the tiny halogen lights that I always want to steal and put in my apartment. *Where do you buy those things?*

I wondered if anyone else was looking up.

Their bluish light highlighted certain points in the room while remaining indifferent about the rest. Some patrons chose the shadowy spots. Today, I chose a table that could have displayed the Hope diamond. It was a small, round pedestal, and the halogen overhead beamed a hot, white light onto the top where a hand-painted image swirled into the center. The diamond now removed, I would give its well-lighted service to my cup of espresso. Very nice.

I pushed my book bag away from the center pole of the table so my feet would have some room and winced at the weight of it. The weight was not a strain for the physical, but for the mental—tons of required reading this week, and I dreaded getting started. I was thankful for the constant distraction of my new environment, and I considered it a welcome duty to continue scanning the room.

The table I slid into was parked in a perfect spot. My back to the rough brick wall, I could see the entrance, the counter, and most of the other tables. Over my left shoulder were the crowded, oversized bookcases that housed countless books, games, old newspapers, and a few items that didn't belong. A polite smile to a few of the other people in my area and all the necessary socializing was over for the moment. The odd collection of art-meets-verbiage on the back wall crowded my mind. Worship, I thought, was a strange topic for a coffeehouse—and a strange subject for the art pieces as well.

Several of the neo-caveman pieces stuck out from the wall about a foot, with a few odd parts trying to reach out a little farther. Each one received a hot little halogen spotlight and screamed "Look at me!"

Pleased to be distracted, I focused on the one closest to me.

Weird. Where did they get that thighbone? It looked real enough to make me wonder. It was hooked up to a phone line and a car battery that were mounted to some sheet metal covered in hieroglyphics. Other techie things and forensic things protruded here and there. Off to one side a roll of printer paper (the kind that had the holes in the sides) looked like it was exploding with the urge to uncoil itself. It was pulled through the teeth of the rollers and mercilessly bolted to the sheet metal. On the first sheet, flattened out for easy viewing, a single short message was hammered out in annoying dot matrix style. I said it over and over again in hopes that the repetition would make it sensible. I turned away from the art piece to pay homage to the beverage in front of me, and I still repeated it.

Trying to move back to my Hope-diamond-replaced-with-espresso-cup fantasy, I imagined that every time I lifted the cup I must quickly replace it with its exact weight in sugar packets to avoid setting off the security alarm. It started to annoy me that I was still repeating that phrase...

In Prayer

Worship

The street I turn from is the busiest in my city. I can still hear the shouting of vendors, the honking of horns, the low drone of the trucks pushing at the back of my collar. I am thankful to be at this intersection today, however, because I am very close to the temple, and afternoon prayer will soon be called. As I enter the broad room I check the sounds of the street at the door, and I am immediately covered with the sound of the loudspeaker from the corner of the building. The phrase is barely intelligible, but after hearing it my whole life it makes sense with or without the words. It is the singsong way that it rolls out over the city that calls us all to prayer and makes each day responsible to remember God.

I unroll my mat. Kneeling on it separates my mind from the pursuits of the day. I think of my prayers, of God, and of my family all at one time. My father died this year, and every time I come to the temple I think of him, but only for a moment, because his memory is always pulling a greater one—a living one—the face of my four-year-old son. I love my son. A sense of deep satisfaction fills my heart because I know I will give to my son what my father gave to me.

My forehead on the ground, I can feel the prayers of the city in my chest. The floor underneath me is firm and unmoving like the tradition of my world. I am at home here—but never quite at rest.

Thoughts
Wonder

No one is in awe of a paper cup.

It is hard to imagine anyone who would be amazed at something so common.

On the other hand, if we, with machetes in hand, cut our way through the deep jungle of some unexplored Pacific Island and found ourselves face to face with humans yet to see the civilized world, we just might have a chance.

Transport: Jungle Scene

After the shock of seeing people with different dress, different color, and different language, and after overcoming the desire to throw us into the Abalooboo Pit, the tribe gathers with nervous excitement around our exploration team leader. Chuck has removed his water bottle from the pack, and, as was his custom to keep from touching the container to his lips, pulls a paper cup from his pack. "Aaaah…ooooh"—the crowd of onlookers inhale, draw back, and then, with wide eyes, move toward the strange new device. Pouring the water into the cup, Chuck says in a matter-of-fact manner, "Cup." After a repeat of the lesson and a wink from Chuck, a few of the tribe attempt the word. By the time he raises it to his lips to finish his drink the whole area is pulsing with the chant, "Cup, cup, cup, cup." We are all backing into the jungle with one eye on Chuck, Possessor of the Cup, and one eye on the painted fellow who is lighting the altar fire and looking our way.

< - - - - - - - - - - -   Transport: Back

Ok, it was a bit cartoonish, but the point is obvious: Things that are new inspire wonder. But where are the new things? Where did wonder go?

Toddlers live in a constant state of wonder. Everything is *new*. Each object is full of new color, shape, weight, and orifice-filling potential. The tragedy of this blissful life is that it will die a slow death with the aging of experience.

Things become *known*.

Secrets are uncovered.

By the time we leave adolescence for adulthood we are threatened with life-killing boredom, having lost all sensation of *wonder* because we can't find anything that is really *new*.

As we grow older we try to find things and activities that will re-engage our sense of wonder. Excitement, however, remains elusive. Euphoria seems to be ruthlessly temporal. The orgasm, by definition, is a momentary experience. The real problem here is not that the experiments of adulthood aren't intensely satisfying, it is that they are only satisfying for a moment. They don't last. Their promise is only for a season. Science, philosophy, and social theory have yet to offer up any vaccines against the dull, aching lack that follows a season of investment in these kinds of faux-wonders.

The answer?

Return to childhood.

What if we could? After all, it was then that everything from a video to a new crayon could amaze us for days, and no laws were broken and no public property was destroyed (well, almost). In childhood, a wooden spoon could entertain us for hours before being discarded for the next wonder-inducing object. Children live in perpetual discovery. It's not that we need to revert to *childishness*—and we certainly can't erase the days of our past— but what if we could find a way to live where there was a constant, ongoing sense of wonder and discovery? What if we could find never-ending entertainment and constant amazement? What if we could embark on an endless adventure and hold an object that was endlessly *novel*?

Novel means new—new to our senses and experience. In novelty there is the excitement of "not knowing" and the rush of discovery. This is the key: to recover the lost joy of childhood we must allow ourselves to slip into the uncomfortable position of *not exactly knowing*. This is not an appeal to become stupid, but it is a confession that we need to interact with things that are beyond our reach. The things that engage our imaginations the most are the things we do not understand: the Bermuda Triangle, alien encounters, the opposite sex, and ghosts, to name a few. They all possess some quality of the Other World—a place where we have never been, but we all seem to know something about.

This place has stirred up our experimentation in religion. Religion, however, is the work of trying to escape the "*not knowing*" by placing quantity, ritual, and form to the mysteries and then marketing the package to others. We have been driven to the inventions of religion, and subsequently we are driven away from religion, by the same internal conviction that *whatever is most worthwhile is ultimately beyond us*. It can't be packaged. Like children, we are obsessed with what we do not have, and we are driven by what we have yet to fully possess. Religion has attempted to help humanity understand the spiritual, but our real need is not to understand the spiritual, or to categorize it, or to explain it—*it is simply to touch it*.

Book after book, movie after movie, and legend after legend tell of how someone has made the Unknown World more understandable for us. Gurus and messiahs are always making the mystical easy and handing it to us in a package. Beware those who explain and categorize. The vast majority of these religious "theories" are in garage sales right now. Many of these revelations have that same wooden spoon quality that inspires the uninitiated for a season and is then thrown to the floor of life. We can memorize it, quote the mantra, and practice the ceremony, but when it has been fully experienced it ceases to enthrall and we have to move on and look for something else.

I believe that it is in the world beyond—the spiritual world—that we will rediscover *wonder*. I believe that in this eternal, other world, that we may find something or someone who is eternally novel—eternally new. We must not settle for theories, temporary things, or religious formulas to interrupt our pursuit…we must find the Endless Novelty and do what is only natural to do…

Java Boy Joe

Vzzzzssshtick. Thub. Thub. Thub. Grinnnnnnnd. The beans bid farewell to their former life and submit to the unforgiving grinding machine. They return as a dark, aromatic powder. This is a good kind of reincarnation. Today the dial on the grinder is set to four, not three, because the air is very humid—odd for Colorado. I pretend I am in Seattle, the Mecca, as I wipe the air off my forehead.

Bangk. Bankgk. Bongk. Swirhhh. The hand-held portafilter gets its head banged against the counter until it coughs up the dark mud, and then the loving altar boy rinses its mouth out under the running water.

Guzz-Tonk-Click-Hmmmm. The new beans are in, back to the mother ship (the hand-held filter has docked), and the wonderful button has been pushed. A moment of silence…and…(Yes!) we are saved. Just in time to keep the buzzing going in my head as I pore over the Introduction to Philosophy text, the Jung addendum, and the flyer on child labor in South America. I am distracted by my need to nurse the cup and by the unusual art pieces hanging on the back wall.

Local artist?

A collection of heavy chain, papier-mâché, the guts of some computer things, *and a bra*. "We've come a long way, baby," I murmur, and glance out the front window. When will labor laws gain any momentum in South America? When will male and female pay scales reach some semblance of equality in North America?

When will they replace that halogen bulb in the three-can lighting track over the diesel-engine-meets-computer-hard-drive-bra art piece? *Blam*! Everything is interrupted by a sudden upheaval in my general area—my table bounces sideways and my bag shoots toward the bookshelf. A girl has tripped over the corner of my book bag and fallen into the guy she was trying to talk to.

I take the interruption as a cue to change my scenery, but not without some protest. I really like this place. I like the familiar smell, and the intriguing visuals are great. I dread exiting to the outside world where nothing is quite as accepting and nothing is quite as focusing. I push the homemade journal and the loose things back into my bag, gather my cup and accessories from their faux altar, and head toward the door. As I push open the door, the cool air helps me mentally reconstruct the art piece I was studying prior to the attack of the tripping couple. Continuing the artist's theme of slapping phrases onto 3-D concoctions, the last piece offered a phrase as well. The engraving read:

RELIGIOUS PEOPLE MAKE TERRIBLE WORSHIPERS

The Circle

Strange Miracle

Thoughts

We all know there is something greater than we are. Whether we consider this fact inside of the physical or non-physical universe, we know it is true. Humankind walks with a sense of hesitant supremacy on the face of the earth. We enjoy our two-legged, upright superiority to other creatures, but we didn't create the world in which we live; it was here before us, and its pre-existence asks some important questions. When we take time to look at our world and our friends we see the most amazingly complex and wonderful collection of molecules and imagination. The question is not just, "How did it all begin?" but "How does it all stay together?" Our faces turn to the sky. What a mystery, to consider how infinitely small we are in comparison to the endless map of the cosmos. Whether we believe the earth is a flat cracker with the sun on a wire, or that we are gravity-sucked onto a blue marble hurling through space surrounded by hot balls of burning gas, the same conclusion must be drawn: *It is a strange miracle that we are alive.*

This strange miracle has translated into a very particular human need throughout all of human history. We need to give credit to the source of all this "living." The hands that were created want to applaud the creator, but first we need to find the author of this miraculous life, look him in the eye, and say, "Oh, it was you!" and then gush with honor and praise for the work. The question, of course, is *just who is he?*

Our desire to honor greatness is not just confined to the heavy discussion of life's origin. Humankind is obsessed with recognizing great things, period. We all want to be in the presence of greatness, and we all want a chance to react to awe-inspiring things. Few people have seen all Seven Wonders of the World. I have seen only one. Recently, I had the privilege of visiting the Taj Mahal. It is an amazing sight, and people travel from all over the world to see it. Entering the booth to pay the entry fee, I was surrounded by German, French, English, and Indian conversations. We were all willing to pay the entry fee because in a few moments we would personally experience something vast, something ancient, something legendary. More than the opportunity to tell the story or show the pictures, there was the anticipation of simply being there and personally responding to the sensory input from such a majestic creation. That is why they are called *Wonders*—that is exactly what they invoke, and that is why we go to experience them—to personally respond to greatness.

It was fantastic to step inside of what I had only seen on television or the printed page. I reveled in the feeling of looking out over the Ganges River toward the farmers with their baskets and camels, the ancient fortress in the distance, and the mist over the river. I wondered how many had stood there before me, over the centuries, with the same impressions. I recounted the incredible story of Shah Jehan's love for his wife and the extra-human effort required to build and adorn such an amazing building. I touched the intricate, colorful stone inlay. It wrapped the entire building. Hundreds of years ago a small, dark craftsman had laid his hands in the same place to set that stone and then continued on in his labor. It was a transcendent, communal event with people from the present and the past around the same inspiring structure; and all the worshipers had taken their shoes off.

If this instinct to touch greatness and engage the awe-inspiring is related to worship, then worship is happening everywhere. People worship in a myriad of places and a myriad of ways. The modern challenge: What inspires my greatest sense of awe and wonder—

in other words, what really deserves my worship? We certainly don't want to worship an object handed to us by some man-made tradition. We refuse to worship out of fear or obligation. We certainly don't want to be led around by Hollywood or religion—neither can be trusted because they sell us objects to worship for their own profit. Regardless of the sometimes confusing choices, our hearts still long to worship and engage the wonderful. So what will we do?

We must choose wisely because the object of our worship will prove our hearts. It proves what is inside of us by the very notion that we would give it honor. Buildings made by men and wonders carved by nature are not great enough to deserve our worship. As we look for something to receive our greatest affection we must make sure that it is truly worthy. If it is not greatly superior to us, then we will be diminished in value. If it does not rest in deep meaning, then it will bring meaninglessness to life. If it does not engage our sense of wonder for eternity, then it is an inferior, temporary object that will impart to us an inferior, temporary sense of being. What we worship has everything to do with how we live, what we love, and what we will become in this life and the life beyond.

In the free market the freedom to choose carries the responsibility to choose wisely. Sometimes we choose the things less promoted because we have personally discovered the product's value. When we have experienced the object of our affection and found it worthy, we no longer need the salesman. Salesmen who try too hard should always be suspect, because a good product sells itself. Whatever is truly worthy of our worship should command our attention with no need for propaganda campaigns. This is where the Strange Miracle of life should enter our discussion. If there is an originator—a supernatural source for our "living"—then this same source should be worthy of intense, exciting, and incredibly meaningful worship! If we find him, he will certainly

need no marketing plan, no propaganda campaign, no handlers, and no image consultants. She would bathe us in wonder, and draw out our worship as naturally as the sun causes the earth to explode with color in the spring.

Will we risk the search?

In Stone

Worship

I see a stone building whose spire seems to reach into heaven itself, calling everyone in the city square to look up, up, up until their necks hurt with the need to see where the spire is pointing. The door at the top of the steps is as tall as the roof on any house in my village, and its welcome is an appropriate introduction to what is inside: an interior so vast, so high, so beautiful that no one from this world could be proud enough to call it their own. Cut stone, gold, silver, brass, woodcarvings, and furniture all exhibit the work of master craftsmen.

Inside the light spills through the windows in a cascade of color and storytelling. I can't read the inscriptions below the stained glass portals but I know their stories well. I know each window, each figure, and parts of each legend come to mind whenever I am near them. I always look to each form in the stained glass and politely nod my appreciation as I remember them. I feel small in this building, under this high ceiling, and I strangely prefer it. When the singing stops and the warm reflections of the sound finally fall underneath the shuffling of feet and the creaking of pews, the priests begin to read out of the book.

This book has the most extraordinary life. It rests unopened in a special gold case at the altar until the priests are prepared to read from it. Then, with the greatest of care, they lift it out and set it on the reading desk. In this moment I think mostly of my low state, and the low state of my affairs, and the specific things I have broken in the rulebook of my heart since last I regretted myself. The book's backdrop is, first, the priest with the most brightly stitched garments; second, the attendants who move silently across the middle of the stage; and third, the enormous golden backdrop—a wall filled with every figure and story and animal and saint I could possibly imagine.

When the book is read I know it is for all of us. I bow my head, others bow their heads, and we listen to the amazing sound. The book is written in the holy language of the priests, and when it is read I cannot understand a word of it. I wonder if anyone else can understand it. I can hardly wait until the priest with the brightly stitched coat explains what is being read. Maybe one of the golden figures will come to life for me in the priest's English words. I touch the dark, rough lapel on my coat and try to loosen the stranglehold that my church clothes have on my neck. I feel small again, and I strangely prefer it.

Fountain Head

Thoughts

Words spring from ideas in the head.

At some point in history an Englishman had an idea in his head about humanity's fixation with greatness and our compulsion to reverence it, and out of his mouth fell the word "worthship." This word speaks of the degrees of worthiness that something or someone might possess. Say "worthship" ten times very quickly and you get "worship."

Understanding value is basic to worship.

Understanding value is the daily work of humanity.

Daily we choose what is important and what is optional, what is precious and what is disposable. We express our own sense of value by how we relate to the things we consider valuable. If we associate with truly great things it reflects how we feel about ourselves. If we give honor to inferior things it reveals an inferior self-concept. Either position will affect the way we relate to the rest of humanity, and to ourselves, and to eternity.

Worship is more than a single activity or concept because activities do not always assign value. It is actually impossible to define any spiritual or emotional truth by using only outward physical expression. To illustrate, we could photograph a person's action and write the caption "This is love" underneath, but we would not have proven the person truly loved the recipient of the action. Can an unloving heart perform an act that appears loving? Sometimes vanity, self-promotion, and obligation make a person do things that might look "loving," but until we see into the heart we cannot come to a firm conclusion. Love is proved by right action *and* right motive, and worship, we will see, is proved the same way.

A "snapshot" of worship activity might reveal someone participating in a religious ceremony. Performing religious rites, ceremonies, and requirements may look like "worship" on the outside, but these things don't prove the heart. Bowing at an altar may bend the person into the "form" of reverence, but the action could be played like an actor's role on a stage. This action might be motivated by fear or obligation. It might just be a cultural habit. If true worship goes deeper than outward performance, what then is the proper inward motivation?

I believe there are two necessary parts to a pure motivation for worship. The first is a deep sense of awe—a heavy realization that we are encountering something very *worthy*. We have seen that humanity, young and old, needs to enjoy great things. This is reflected in the joy of childhood wonder and the pursuit of adulthood pleasures. We all need to experience wonder, and we instinctively want to give honor to the things that inspire it in us. This is the idea of "worthship," and it is intensely relevant to our search for excellent worship. If it is not deeply worthy—if it does not evoke awe—it should not receive our worship.

The second part of our motivation to worship is related to our *love* for the object worshiped. Love is the prime mover of humanity, and if we are going to bow and reverence something great, then please let it be something we love.

Love.

What a huge word! To discover how love motivates worship we might first ask, "What do we love?" In writing out our answers, however, the question will lose its potency, because it has the answerable equivalent of "What things are good?" There will be as many answers as there are mouths to speak them because we use these words "love" and "good" so loosely.

Maybe a better question is, "What loves me?"

Discovering "What loves me?" creates a list of things that are capable of loving us in return. This question will protect us from trivializing the word. We can't include inanimate objects on our list because they can't return love. We have to cross out activities and concepts because they can't love as well. We can't even include great people or powerful gods if they have not proven their love for us. If we are to worship anything or anyone, then *please let them love us first.* Would we counsel a woman to remain in relationship with an abusive, unloving partner? Of course not. We all know that a woman trapped in an abusive relationship is not only *being broken*, but she is also demonstrating her own *brokenness* by remaining in the "relationship." We demonstrate the same odd brokenness if we are caught worshiping any entity that has not proven its love for us. Pure love toward us requires a pure love in return.

We cannot consider *being loved* in the same way we say that we love our favorite sweatshirt. The sweatshirt has no heart, no history, and will make no demands of us. We might offer this trivial kind of "love" to a sweatshirt, but we require others to love us in a very different way. We have a heart (it can be broken); we have a history (some of it not so good); we are often very demanding. We need a grand, legendary love just to deal with us. We are also convinced that it will take a miracle for someone to truly love us because we can scarcely love ourselves. When someone comes along and, after seeing all of us—the good, the bad, and the ugly—still offers unconditional love, we treasure them like no other! This is the kind of love we could freely celebrate. This is the kind of love that could earn a lifetime of return. Simply put, legendary love motivates the sweetest kind of wonder, and inspires the purest return of love. So as we seek to worship well, we must find a worthy, loving object.

I believe a legendary love sweeps through eternity, and that love is written like poetry on the hands of the divine. When we discover it we will be swept along into the arms of the most loving and awe-inspiring...

Goat's Milk

Java Boy

The sweet smell was not exactly pleasant, nor was it particularly offensive. And it was definitely not the smell of tea.

I had been in India on a cultural exchange from the university for about three weeks. Every morning I would wander downstairs, nod at the hotel attendants, glance over the newspapers in search of a headline in English, and settle back into one of the firm, straight couches in the lobby. It only took a moment for one of the young Indian men to offer a tray filled with tea or coffee. Sugar, spoons, cups, carafe, and waxy paper napkins. I liked the tea, but this morning I ordered coffee. Well, almost coffee. Nescafe. Brewed in goat's milk, this insta-beverage is not quite centered on the tongue. It was curious enough to make me order it again.

The room was large, with marble floors and marble columns. An ancient-feeling room, with not-so-ancient furnishings. Some *bas-relief* wall hangings covered in plastic, a wooden reception desk, and various couches and end tables purchased from local vendors. In the middle of the room stood a statue that was part elephant and part woman, with an almost-fresh flower necklace around its brass neck and a small tray in the front filled with ashes—the source of the pungent smell.

I was not sure of his name, but I was sure of his devotion to this particular activity. He was about the hotel all day, but he never seemed to be doing anything except in the morning—around this statue. Every person in India seemed to have a very particular job, and they were quite given to it. One man opens the door. One woman sweeps the floor. One man takes your order. One man carries the bags. One man brings the tea. One man completes the form. My travel companions had a running argument over this man's particular duty. No one could prove anything except this: He worshiped the figurine.

Specifically, he held some burning incense sticks in his hands, gestured toward the statue, turned in a circle, mumbled some prayers, gestured the incense toward his head, turned in a circle (a few more repetitions), and then placed the burning smells in the small holder in front of the statue. Every morning. Every day. It was hard *not* to watch, and this had me off balance. My instinct wanted to turn away from this private, religious exercise. I felt like a voyeur of the tourist kind, but I was not prohibited from watching the public act, and I was so close I felt as if I were *made* to participate. My nose was certainly participating. The man paid no attention to me as he humbled himself in front of the strange statue.

From behind the paper I tried to appear as if I was paying no attention to him. It reminded me of seeing two attractive people kissing in public. I should turn away, but my eyes always want to discover what is going on. Have they just reunited after a long journey? Are they married? Do they know people are watching? I tried to bury my interest in the headlines on the page in front of me and drank the rest of my coffee.

In my mind, these morning "encounters" are now combined in a twisted mental image inspired by the techno-cave art I had seen at Café Mystique. My imaginary art piece features one of the phrases from the back wall of the coffeehouse:

Worship In Philosophy

The smoke from my pipe swirls around my head and up through the bookshelves on the wall behind me. It snakes through the texts from Nietzsche, Darwin, Asimov and over the dog-eared essays of Dawkins, Hume, and Sagan. These are the words of wonder. The collection is covered with the memories of all the years I spent mastering the maze of academic achievement, and now the subsequent years I spend setting the maze for others who dare to enter.

My favorite mice are the freshmen classes that come in wide-eyed, still covered in the crumbs of their half-baked theories of life. Barely out of the high chair of religion, they can't even chew real intellectual food. It never ceases to amaze me: the number of kids who still try to prove that there is a God. I will pull their bad teeth and give them a taste of the solid food of solid intellects.

I remember the poster stapled to the kiosk in the Commons that read, "God, Deliver Us From Your Followers!" I nod in assent and briefly run though a few memories of my own undergrad activism, then I tamp the tobacco and relight.

My graduate school students have come a long way. For them I work very hard, day and night, providing more fuel for the fire, more words for the argument, more illustrations to debunk the absurdity.

At the moment, however, I enjoy the peace of my world.

I run my hand along the edge of the heavy desk and organize the stack of recent papers from my Freshman Comparative Religion course. Soon I will have to deal with each submission piece by piece, precept by precept, and with every stroke of my correction try to bring some level of enlightenment to the masses. I engage both admirers and dissenters. I appreciate conviction, but I welcome the chance to challenge narrow-minded religious types.

Staring out the window too long while enjoying the introspection, I burn a greenish splotch into my vision. I have to squint for a while to relieve the temporary blindness. Knocking the remainder of the ashes into the tray, I can barely hear the sounds of the neighbor kids playing ball next door, the phone ringing in the other end of the house, and my wife calling me to lunch. In the afternoon we will take the convertible to the hills and enjoy the warming of spring. I push the papers into a stack on the corner of my desk and tell myself they will be done by Monday—no problem.

Tenure is good.

The Dark Brother

Our internal, supernatural urge begs for exercise. When released to maturity it practices worship. Worship begins as a simple human reflex—an instinct to honor greatness. To say that worship is one of our human instincts may sound a bit strange, but it is no less true. It might be best understood by examining three related internal capacities: love, dreams, and worship.

First, we should reject the notion that an internal capacity that is practiced poorly is a false practice altogether—or that it is not an instinct. Is love an inborn human capacity? How do we know? Is it from witnessing perfect love throughout the world that we know humans are most *human* when they operate in love? Hardly. We may point to the Mother Teresas of the world to example love, but we all know that standing behind her in the crowd are a hundred selfish, unloving thoughts. What we also know, however, is that our hearts resonate with approval when we witness true love, and when we commit love we feel a deep connection with something important and lasting. Love is a necessary instinct.

How do we know that dreams are mandatory to humanity? Dreaming in this context is not what we pursue when we sleep. This is the practice of imagining the beautiful future to come— when we are awake. Dreaming is living the future hope in the present imagination. Sometimes we use the term to denote some- one who has their "head in the clouds" and has lost touch with reality, but in contrast, we would never aspire to live without a dream for the future. We know when humanity is in full swing that it dreams *great* dreams. Martin Luther King Jr. inspired us with his, but we all want to have one of our own. Dreaming is an instinct.

How do we know that worship is human requirement? People are desperately trying to love and be loved in every nation on earth, but not all are doing it well. There are dreamers all over the world, but not everyone dreams well. It may be difficult to see all people worshiping well, but it, like love and dreams, is a non-negotiable human work. People worship things great and small, some half-heartedly and some with manic obsession. Children are overwhelmed with their adoration for every new thing, and adults are building new "temples of worship" in every city of the world. We look for great things to admire and eternal things to honor. Worship is one of our most common exercises. Worship is an instinct.

Secondly, something's absence often proves the needful reality of its presence. Like two lovers separated for a time, the absence not only makes the heart grow fonder, it also helps each discover what they really need in each other. These internal things—love, dreams, and worship—prove in their absence that they are most necessary, for when they are gone something terrible happens to humanity. When they are gone something dark fills the vacuum of their absence. This awful displacement is parallel to the nature of *dark* and *cold*. In the absence of light comes dark, but darkness has no life of its own. Light is something, but dark is simply the nothing that fills the space when light is gone. In the absence of heat, cold is ushered in, but cold has no presence; it is simply nothing waiting for heat's return.

When love is gone it leaves an awful replacement. It is not *hate*, because hatred is a targeted, active passion that can co-exist with love in the same life. Love's vacuum is filled with *indifference*. Indifference will not share the room with love. Love wants to act; indifference wants to lie down. Love wants to rescue; indifference turns the channel. Love demands selflessness; indifference cares for no one enough to call the "self" away from its own pursuits. Indifference, not hatred, would destroy humanity in a short season if love were completely removed from the earth.

If dreams were banished we would be left with a simple, pathetic *existence*. Existence is survival with no reason to celebrate. Dreams fly high in the heart of humanity and build in us the hope for a future, the ability to innovate, and the strength to endure present difficulty. Existence, on the other hand, looks down at the ground, regrets the past, stumbles along into the future, changes nothing, and dies with a whimper.

The absence of worship leaves a space for something sinister as well. Worship's vacuum fills with *pride*. Now pride is the black hole of human potential: *pride* becomes *pride* becomes *pride*. Pride will not bow, it will not honor another, and it will not believe in anything higher. Worship, in high contrast, is humility that has found a higher thing to reverence, it has discovered the joy of inferiority, and it has made an art of offering thanks, honor, and affection to something greater. Worship is humility that has matured. Without worship humankind is reduced to embrace itself as the jewel of its own pursuits, like a dog chasing its tail, and pride will prove its destructive intent.

In the end, a life full of love and dreams will soar into the future while those tied to the stake of indifference and existence are pulled to the ground and forgotten. Likewise, the life full of worship will find itself lifted up, carried beyond itself, while wingless pride plummets into a lonely hole of self-obsession.

At this point it is difficult *not* to conclude that the capacity to love, dream, and worship all point to some great spiritual reality. It is not a distant leap. Something eternal continues to challenge us to these three high human expressions, which all seem to extend from another realm. It is not DNA, physics, or theories of probability that give birth to and sustain these three mysterious instincts. They could not have originated from the cells of our bodies any more than our will or our laughter, and that is a comforting fact. It means there is more to life than meets the natural eye. There is hope beyond the relentless, tangible world, and it seems to have taken serious interest in depositing something of itself in all of us.

These three instincts are the tell-tale signs of a benevolent, transcendent force.

It is this undeniable deposit that points us to the fact that there should be a *God*.

And there is more to believing in this kind of God than causality. There is more than reason or theory. There is more than feeling, tradition, or faith. There is *life itself*. "I think, therefore I am" is woefully inadequate to express the true nature of human life. If there is life worth living there will be love, dreams, and worship—not just *thinking*. And these three point to something *divine*.

Love for expressing the sweetest part of relationship.

Dreams for pressing far beyond temporary material existence.

Worship for personally interacting with the transcendent source of it all.

The Outer Realm

Through Nature

Something is pursuing us. Something is peeking at us from behind the door. Someone is writing scripts for a few of our thoughts. There is someone staging an occasional dream sequence. Someone is ringing a bell, and we have heard it before—but we can't say when or where.

Standing at the edge of the Worship Circle we begin to realize something very subtle, but very far-reaching. We realize that we are not personally responsible for having come to this point. Someone from beyond has been dealing with us. He has been calling to us. He has been dropping clue after clue on the field of our life, hoping we might pick up the trail. Those clues are beginning to fall together into a story—a narrative of His pursuit.

And here we are.

Without stepping in any farther we can walk around the Circle and take notes from all the people who are here with us. We can journal our own experiences and those of others and find this to be true: We may have come to touch God, but He has been trying to touch us all along.

From this point each step in the journey depends on our decision to go deeper into the mystery of eternity and the mystery of worship.

How deep will we go?

Something supernatural reaches out to us through *nature*.

If there was really a Creator who created the earth and the universe, then where did He get the materials? Did He run down to the corner store and search the section marked "Materials for Creation" and max his card on a purchase? Just where were the materials for creation found? If they were in existence before Him, then who created them?

If there is a Divine Power, then by definition He must be not be preceded, outdone, or outrun. He must be all, and in all.

In all?

Creation came from the Creator, but He did not reach outside of Himself for the materials because nothing existed beside Him. The creator would have reached into Himself and drawn the brush of His imagination through an endless palette of color. Turning in a dance of creative expression, He released the universe, the earth, mankind, and all of our known world into existence.

He must be expressed in everything He made.

Some ancient literature says, "For since the creation of the world God's invisible qualities—his eternal power and divine nature—have been clearly seen, being understood from what has been made, so that men are without excuse [to not know Him]." This must be true for two simple reasons. If the Divine created the world then His imagination is displayed for us, just as the imagination of any artist is displayed in his work. Second, since He could not use materials outside of Himself, the very medium of His creativity reflects His nature because it all found its origin in Him. Both the paint and the Painter are clearly displayed in creation.

One of the secrets to becoming a great worshiper is to learn to feel the Creator touching us through nature. He reveals Himself through it. The same ancient insights that point us to His presence also point us to our difficulty: We can't always see Him very clearly. Something has happened to our vision. We are standing small, in the center of a great forest, and we can't see the forest because of the trees. We need help, and we need practice, to develop spiritual eyes—eyes that can see into the heavens. With some effort and some special exercises it can be done.

Here is a seven-day, seven-step path to finding His touch in nature. This path can be repeated like a cycle, over and over, until the Divine is better seen and understood. Each activity will take a dedicated moment, but a relatively short one. We can take our time. These experiments can be improvised and adapted at any point. Like other Paths of Seven outlined in this book of spiritual experiments, these are only one small part of the whole adventure. You do not need to complete them all before you read on.

1. Take a walk. Find a wide, open place. Look at the sky and turn to scan the entire horizon. Say out loud, "The Creator is big." Ask Him to speak to you about how big, and spend a few moments considering the thoughts that enter your mind.

2. Find a tree. Hold a leaf in your hand. Look at the intricacies of the leaf. Consider the greater intricacy of your own hand. Consider the priority of the heavenly artist. What did He spend the most time on? What does this say about Him? What does this say about you?

3. Take a walk. Find a spot where no one is looking. Jump up and down. Consider the sound your stomping makes, the way your feet feel, the thoughtless but trustworthy nature of gravity, and the way your breathing speeds up to handle the fun. Ask the Creator, "Did You have fun putting all this together?" Consider your thoughts.

4. Get on the Internet and search the Web for "Natural Disasters." Find some photos of catastrophe. Say out loud, "If Nature is God, then who needs Her?" Shake your fist. Now ask the Power behind the natural, "Why do these things happen?" Spend a few minutes considering what His heart is saying to yours.

5. Look around your immediate world. How many colors do you see? How many colors are there in the world you can't see right now? It's too much to think about really. Consider the endless colors that must be present in the Great Artist, and the endless ways He sees to use them. Try to give Him credit for being so expressive.

6. Plan a private viewing of a sunrise or a sunset. Watch for something unique. In a very normal, personal way give the Great Artist a running commentary on what you love about the moment. Be sure to offer specific compliments and note appreciation for the fine details of the event. Feel free to go on and on.

7. Remember your favorite pet. Or remember your favorite encounter with an animal. Fond memories? Why did the Creator make so many animals? What does the complexity of the animal kingdom reveal about Him? Consider your love for certain animals and your fear of others. Ask Him to show you the meaning of the differences.

The Machine

Java Boy

Some might say that in the purchase of an espresso machine, part of the magic has been given away. Like putting a mountain in a glass globe with swirling fake snow, something essential is lost. Whatever. I wanted more. Punished with weird "Joe" in India for months, I was up for selfishness. Besides, my university budget was getting tighter and I decided to invest in practicality.

Maybe I had given up the long lines and the cost of someone else shooting the steam through a handful of coffee beans. Maybe I had given up the coffeehouse community experience, but what I gained was not a trade but an option. I could go. I could stay. Either way I could have my Joe.

One of the benefits to the upgrade was becoming the resident coffee guru in my circle of friends. I could stand in the kitchen and make insightful statements about the nature of man's most exciting beverage, and gesture, not to some unrelated point in the room, but directly toward the Machine. Yes. View the mystery. Grinding. Tamping. Drawing. All the while I'm spouting secret knowledge and mysteries unknown to the owner of the drip machine. Espresso fantasies of grandeur.

The highest illustration for my transition might be in the parallel between lust and love, drip and steam. Make sure you understand the comparison properly to avoid any inappropriate visuals. Lust should give way to its superior: love. Drip should bow to its master: steam. I have moved from teenage infatuation and unsatisfying experimentation to the mature, intimate relationship of espresso.

Today I had pushed to the next level in my relationship. I had done what some try to do with peyote. In my desire to find the right blend of beans I had thrown back seven or eight double shots, with sugar. I do not recommend the experience. It is probably dangerous. I knew something was awry when the portafilter, held in my trembling hand, rattled against the Machine as I approached it with the next load. I was audibly talking myself through the process like the air traffic controller over the radio to the disoriented pilot:

"Come in Java Boy, come in…can you read me? Focus your eyes Java Boy, we've got work to do!"

Now that I have admitted that I have a problem I am better able to deal. I now focus more on the communal and entertainment value of my gift. We play Spades, Speed Scrabble (a variation for the caffeinated), and, if the Northern friends are present, we commit Euchre. I have framed a small reminder that hangs directly above the Machine to keep my motives intact and my usage under control. It reads (leaning away from the overhead light reflection): "Espresso Is Connection." This refers not to a connection with the world induced by hallucinogens, but the world of connections with people—the people I am getting to know over the beverage, the people I love who share the same cup, and the people I can impress with my coffee-making art.

I stole the idea for the framed reminder. The psycho-art pieces from the often-visited café in the cultural district stayed with me like stowaways in the mind. The one piece that seemed to beg for superiority among all the others was not actually in the center of the wall as I remembered it, but mounted a bit too high. I stood under it on my solo trip to the facilities and used my "waiting for a turn" as an excuse to examine it more closely. Its use of snake-skin, mannequin head, and satellite dish was very loud, but they competed with one of those scrolling banner things where the red letters roll from right to left over the multi-bulbed surface. This banner thing demanded attention and it balanced the shouting from the rest of the work. Over and over it scrolled the same message. I had modified the message for my present need, but it originally read:

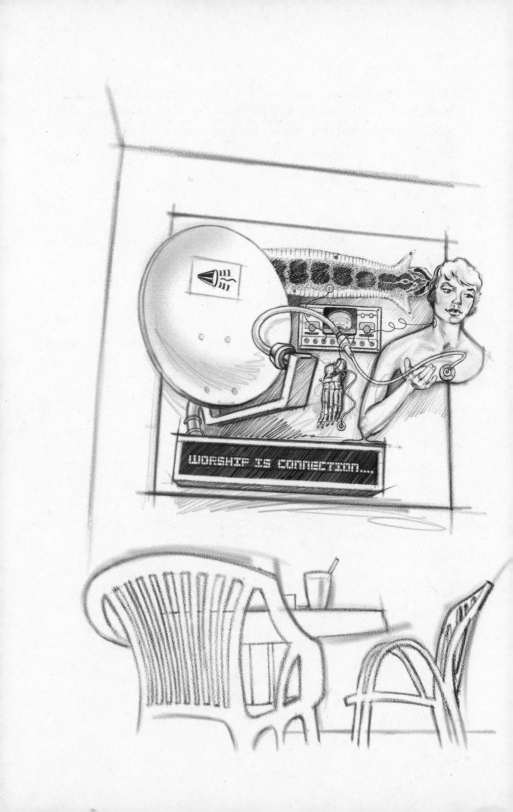

Considering Thoughts

Religious people think it's enough to participate in worship-like activity. Most religious people spend a lifetime learning the intricacies of their worship traditions, but they never love the object of their worship. What a farce! No wonder religion in the Western hemisphere has hit the bottom of the cultural barrel—it has proven itself to be an exercise in foolishness. Westerners have settled for the gesture of worship over the object of worship. In the East, religious people worship everything. Gods that have never demonstrated any loving interaction with humankind are still revered and honored, and the religion of "one-way effort" is seldom questioned as inadequate.

The *anti-religious* have used these foolish pictures of worship activity as a basis for their protest. It just may be that their anti-sentiment has been birthed on an undeniable truth that only they have had the courage to shout: There is nothing attractive about doing religious things that, in the end, point to nothing beyond the "things" themselves. We all despise the pretense of a marriage that shares a checkbook, a car, and a house, but refuses to share any sort of intimate, honest relationship—we should be free to despise the same pretense in religion. We need a God worthy of worship, not religious activity.

Many *irreligious* people spend a lifetime avoiding all the trappings of religion, but in the process they also have removed themselves from any conversation with the supernatural. Philosophy, whether formal or armchair, is fun for the mouth but no fun for the heart if it does not lead to something higher, something eternal. Do we have to count the number of famous philosophers in the modern era who died in twisted disillusionment because thinking without truly living was death? There is nothing admirable about someone who tries to live well in the physical and intellectual realms, while crippling the spiritual realm with denial. No wonder intellectuals have been walking with a limp.

Spiritualists dabble in everything weird and powerful, but have yet to point to an entity worthy of worship. Automatic writing and channeling a spirit guide is exciting, but does either one contain a lasting, valuable connection with the transcendent? Is the quality of our lives enhanced through an occasional brush with the paranormal? Are we any better off—are we any better loved—after a token encounter with the mystical?

Maybe we should avoid cynicism and try to lean into a new realism. The new realism might say that we don't have to throw out any of these expressions as completely illegitimate, because each may have something important to offer. A bit of religion is probably good because it prods us to consider eternal things. Some anti-religion might keep us sober to the fact that people constantly misunderstand God. Some irreligion might serve us like a good glass of wine: relax and enjoy the humor of life. Spiritualism might provide a release to experience firsthand the reality of the transcendent—not just sit around and talk about it. All of these expressions may deserve some room in our experience, but the challenge here picks up where they leave off.

There is another step.

I believe we must move forward and find a permanent connection to the supernatural.

We must find a way to adventure in the supernatural and redefine our present physical reality with something more permanent.

We must find a way to have a conversation with God so we will better understand the possibility of eternity and our own inevitable future.

Worship is the key to this connection.

Through the window of worship an atheist has the unique opportunity to be a voyeur to the World Beyond, but he will have to suspend his tradition of disbelief. Through worship modern mystics may enter into a more permanent exchange with what has only been an occasional encounter, but they may have to look deeper than the surface of the supernatural. The Easterner may find relief from the endless wheel of self-improvement and indifferent deities at the gentle hands of a worthy and loving God. The Westerner, through experiential worship, will find reason to leave judgment of all things supernatural at the door. Human reason can sometimes ruin a dinner party with the divine. Worship can free the lovers of religion from the pride that has bound their hands and taped their mouths.

There must be a God who is worthy of worship. The question is now: Will we find Him?

Worship
In Tradition

Finding a seat was never that difficult.

Fourth from the back, left side, by the wall. It was mine unless some untrained visitor decided to hide his family away in that particular pew.

Most of the talking and singing is now a drone in my head. I think about many things as I stand up and sit down, but I don't think of the activity any more than I would think of moving my legs when I walk. I look at my thumb, squeezing on the bottom center of the hymnal to keep it open while we sing. I look at the girl who is singing the solo and think to myself, *She's cute.* She did not seem quite as attractive when she grimaced to reach the high notes. Clapping ensues, partly in reverence for her courage and partly to provide noise for her stage-left exit. Down the three carpet-covered steps, across in front of the piano she glides. The guest speaker makes an attempt to greet her on his way up to fill her previous position. She careens past his gesture, however, so focused on escaping the stage that she doesn't see him until the last moment. She bounces around his shoulder, turns one of her heels slightly sideways in the carpet, and covers her mouth with her hand as she spins onto the front row among her friends.

After some pleasantries the speaker is going at us with all the alliteration, rhyme, gesture, and forehead-mopping he can muster. We return mostly blank stares, but there is one low voice and one high voice in the audience using words like "amen" or "that's right" in response to his points—much to his satisfaction. I have made some profound doodling on the back of the offering envelope by the time the whole congregation leans forward for the closing prayer. As I lean forward, avoiding eye contact with the speaker, I rest my head on the wooden bench in front of me. I can smell the musty hymnal pages, I can see my feet and the feet next to me, and my stomach squeezes out a warning about lunch. The preacher has begun to beg us to come to the altar and make a public decision to agree with him, or to join the church, or to confess our sins, and the list goes on for a while. I think through my options, retire a few of the appeals as obsolete or non-applicable, and decide to quietly sit this one out.

Shaking hands with the pastor and the speaker on the way out, I squint at the brightness of the sun. I watch one of the men extinguish a cigarette off the side of the front porch and see my parents opening the doors of the family car. My stomach is very happy. The dinner table is less than ten minutes away.

Seven
Through People

A human touch can be very nice. Hard days, even hard weeks, can be brought to a careful resolve through a single, loving touch. The question for the searching heart is whether the touch is entirely human, or if it just might contain something else...

Like a message from beyond, a story is being told by the birth, life, and death of humanity. The sights, sounds, and touches of the people we contact are of no small consequence in discovering the Creator. If He has painted any one thing that is closer to "self-portrait" than any other work, it is the masterpiece of "us." We are individually and collectively the most complex, advanced, and masterful creation in the known universe. Careful thought must have been given to each of us.

Each human being reveals volumes about the One who set them in motion, and together we sing a chorus of information. We don't have to look for angelic beings or mysterious people. The ordinary will do just fine. They can be near or far away from us. The key is having eyes to see through them into the mind of the Creator. We should not, however, assume that humanity's *actions* are a window into the complete character of their Creator. People do not work like robots, and the sum of their actions do not represent their inventor. In other words, God might not be known by all of humanity's choices, but He might always be found in their ability to choose.

God has been touching us through people. Here is a Path of Seven that can help open up this reality.

1. Watch someone walk. Millions of neural commands and the physical expressions of motion, balance, momentum, and reaction all coordinate into one very ordinary act: walking. People can go where they want to and move how they will. What does this reveal about their Creator? What does it reveal about us that we never notice the gift of ability, but only what we accomplish with it?

2. Remember that hand on your shoulder? The affirming touch with no words spoken? What a speech is made into our hearts when someone who cares touches us in an affirming, non-threatening way. Consider how vulnerable people are to the sense of touch. Consider the difference between being touched by an inanimate object, like a tree, and an animal— and then being touched by a person.

3. Consider the troubled peoples of Africa or Eastern Europe or Los Angeles—a collection of complex tragedies. Where is God in all the death, anger, disease, and war? Is He tied up somewhere? Is He standing and approving? Ask God to show you where He is, and look for a personal answer.

4. Take a picture of a loved one to a quiet place where no one is watching. Hold the picture up so that the sky is its backdrop. Say aloud, "You are deeply valuable to me, and you were not an accident. You can never be replaced." Pause and enjoy the moment. Many scientists say that humans are just complex organic accidents. Do you need something more to be said? Who will say it?

5. Take a small mirror to a quiet place where no one is watching. Hold the mirror and find your face in it. Let the sky be your backdrop. Listen for God to say, "You are deeply valuable to me, and you were not an accident. You can never be replaced." Did you hear it? Is there someone else who would say it for Him? Say it yourself, aloud. Does it feel right?

6. Consider sex. What a fabulous and troubling thing! We can't re-create without it, but the non-creative, recreational version seems to be just a little less fulfilling than the advertisements promised. The act can be both fulfilling and unfulfilling. "God, why did You create sexuality? Are You the God of pleasure? Are You the God of family? Are You the God of intimacy? Pain?"

7. What has been the most important thing in your life? What has had the most ability to bring pleasure and pain? Was the answer wrapped up in a person? It almost always is. Consider what our relational core says about the essence of the God who designed us.

The Mountain

There are many paths to the top of a mountain.

I was soon to learn that at the top of the highest mountains the paths would often converge into one singular, impossible way.

Mountains are real, and so are people, and so is the cold, and so is God. Why people continue to die struggling to the top of the Himalayan peaks used to offend my sense of reason, but not so much anymore. Experience changes things. In short, an experience with God changes everything.

No, I have not climbed K-2 or Everest, but I have been to the Mountain and the experience is superior to the climbing of the smaller ones in Asia—except for the fact that they are not quite as deadly.

My journey was inspired by the same power that inspires most others to climb—I had grown unsatisfied with the low altitude of my life and I began to have dreams of the summit.

I had grown tired of jogging around the block—feeling the burn in my legs, pushing past the tightness in my chest—only to pass the green front door of my own familiar home again and again and again. People can say there is no use in trying to escape low altitude. They can ridicule the rebellious for leaving the "easy" in pursuit of the "difficult," but at least the rebels enjoy change, and the dreamers always seem to go *somewhere*.

I was tired of the mouse wheel. I had to get off.

There was more to living than the redundant wheel of material things and material ideas. There was something deeper, something greater, and it was pounding in my ears. If the pounding was just the sound of my heart, I could have stayed home. It was not. It sounded more like the pounding rhythm of a hammer, and it was ringing on the anvil of my life. In a waking vision I saw the hammer arc through the air, and then I saw, without a doubt, that it was held in the hand of God.

I was not particularly angry nor particularly philosophical. I could accept my mortality, but I would like to know what He was thinking when He made me—and I thought I deserved to know. If I could just hold His face in my hands, then I would take the time to look deep; I would find some answers. After a long look I could choose whether to kiss or slap, but first I had to *find* Him.

Part of the internal drive to climb comes from some unseen force that wants to act without reason or plan. It is grossly related to the urge to dive off tall buildings just to spite gravity. The relationship has something to do with the unreasonable nature of the pursuit. Another, more benevolent, motivator is the Legend.

People talk.

I was old enough to hear others speak of the great mountain, the view, and of those who had made it to the summit. I wanted to be part of the story. I fantasized about returning from the Mountain with inspiring tales and rare experience. I wanted to be a storyteller. I wanted to live in the Legend. At the time, however, my story was the wheel of things—how it went round and round and round.

I bought a copy of the Legend—a collection of stories about the lives and adventures of people who lived to reach the Mountain, and of those who had refused to go. I wasn't far into the book when I found a story of one of the mountain climbers who had made the summit. He, too, began his journey with frustration and anger, trapped in the wheel of things. He pushed for the summit while pursuing the voice of God. I was pursuing the same voice, I thought, because I knew I could not stay where I had been. I was suffocating in the crowd of valley dwellers who did not believe in the Mountain, the pursuit, or the God who might speak to us if we made it to the top.

This character in the Legend was able to talk with God when they were on the Mountain. I believed it was true. This is what I wanted. I hung a picture of the Mountain in my living room and thought about it every day. I thought about it at work, I thought about it in my sleep, and I thought about it when I sat and stared at it from across the room. I wondered if others could see my thoughts—they seemed to be bold enough to raise the letters on my forehead: I want to see God!

My body was in serious need of preparation. My mind needed serious convincing that my body could even do it. My inner conviction, however, did not waiver: I was going to make it to the top. I began to focus my life on the make-ready.

First, I rented every video and read every book I could find on mountain climbing. I learned about other climbers' pursuits, and it helped me refine my own plan. Their failures and successes helped me plot my course.

I was beginning to understand that in the range of high pursuits there are many different mountains. From childhood I had been told, in fairy tales, that many paths lead to the top of a mountain. That might be true for some mountains, but had they been to the highest ones? Had the writers of fairy tales been to the top of *the* Mountain? Well, I could read a map, and it was easy to see that across the great mountain ranges there were dozens of hills, peaks, and plateaus. Some were much higher than others, and the highest would be almost impossible to climb. Some had vicious reputations, while some invited almost everyone to their summits.

I noticed that many of the lower mountains were covered with wide roads leading to the top—wide enough for busloads of tourists. The top of these mountains held monuments commemorating the masses of people who had been there. They had purchased tiny flags at the summit gift shop and placed their tokens into the soil of their achievement. The highest mountains were rarely climbed and scarcely marked. I knew instinctively that the easy, tourist mountains were not my call, and it would be on the highest of the peaks that I would meet my destiny. It would be there I would meet God.

I ran farther, I ate better, I slept more, and I kept a diary of my training experience. I was setting goals, pursuing them one step at a time, and my body was submitting to the work. Each goal was a little higher than the last, and each one demanded that I give up something more from my previous life as I pursued higher altitude. I had no idea that as my life filled with the effort to reach God, all the new activities would simply displace the old. Some of the new activities were poured into the vacuum of my sofa-induced nothingness, killing off wasted effort and meaningless ideas. Some of the training created brand-new areas of discipline. I was beginning to see better and breathe the air with a greater sense of confidence.

I had always been told by valley-dwellers that to achieve the summit of the great Mountain one had to give up everything dear and meaningful in life. This was an unwelcome proposition for most, and it kept most people from attempting the climb, but I had nothing to lose. Captured by the opportunity to hear the voice of God, I never even thought to weigh my pathetic life against the object of my pursuit. I was obsessed with the goal and gave very little thought to the price I would pay.

I sold off the clutter in the garage and replaced it with well-

organized climbing gear. I swept the seldom-read books, magazines, and bizarre trinkets from the bookshelves of my study into
the fireplace for kindling, and I replaced the useless stuff with
new things. I covered the shelves with accounts of climbing failure and success, magazines on related climbing topics, and
photo albums logging my own training progress.

I dissolved some savings accounts that were doing nothing for
anyone, sold some dead stock, and invested in some high-risk
funds related to the service industry. They earned quick returns
that helped me save for the enormous cost of the trip, and they
helped others at the same time. I liked it. I missed very little of
what I had once held dear. Oh, I still loved people, and I still
loved my distant family, but how I loved them was beginning to
change. My sense of value was being completely rearranged, and
my life was coming into an amazing order that made me question
what I had been doing before I pursued the Mountain.

This was about the time that I met Chris. She was a mountain
climber. She was a seeker. She had climbed the Mountain, she
had made the summit, and she had touched the face of God.
Honestly, I didn't believe it at first. She did not seem like a
climber, and she did not appear to have the strange religious
shape that the valley-dwellers always drew in their caricatures of
seekers. She was strangely normal in appearance, and I liked
being with her.

When we first met we talked of all sorts of things like our fami-
lies, our jobs, and our other friends. I learned quickly that Chris
carried the Legend in her, but she was not compelled to tell the
story in every conversation. Sometimes I think she avoided the
subject so as not to be mistaken for a salesperson. So, to have it
my way, I would always bring it up.

Fears and uncertainties would still jump out of my head like
sleeping reflexes, and they made me sound like an awkward

skeptic. She seemed to recognize these convulsions as involuntary and took no offense. My own passion flickered in my eyes when I asked her to tell me more of her adventures: How long did it take? How did you prepare? What was He like? We filled many evenings in front of the fire, many times with a circle of her friends and mine, telling our stories, asking our questions, and even confessing our failures and fears. We read from our copies of the Legend and discussed what it all seemed to mean for us as modern climbers.

Soon we started climbing together. Small faces, easy mountains. Chris was very good, and I soon learned that she had a lot to give me and that she enjoyed the giving. I think that in the back of both of our minds was a picture of the Mountain—mine in my living room and hers in her memory. It wasn't long into our experiences together that I told her of my obsession to reach past the material world and touch the face of God. I verbalized the confession in the form of a question: "Chris, would you help me to climb the Mountain?"

There are many maps and climbing guidebooks. The oldest map I had was yellowed and ragged around the edges. I had stored it away in a trunk in the attic since I was a boy, and I had never once thought about it until now. Pulling it out I could see that it covered a grand old range in the East where many had traveled in the past, but few ventured anymore. Little holes were torn open at the corners of all the tightest folds. I carefully unfolded the ancient map in front of Chris and watched as her fingers drew a path across the signposts and markers to what I had never seen clearly before.

It was huge. It was ominous. I think it actually scared me. It made all the other mountains appear as bumps on the surface of the earth, and I understood, without thought, that this was the

Mountain. This was the summit. On the highest point of this monstrous challenge a single word was inscribed beside a tiny dot that read "Altar to the Living God." We stood for a while, quiet, and when I finally broke the silence I stumbled through my words to express one simple thought: *This is where we are going.*

To do the high places a guide is indispensable. Chris told me there would be times on the highest places when an expert guide would visit me and speak direction to my heart in ways she never could. It was a puzzling statement, but I had grown to trust everything she said. We had climbed some very difficult peaks together, and she had saved me more than once when I failed to anchor a pin or tie a line off properly. It was too late to question the spiritual nature of our conversation or the spiritual part of my endeavor. They were now firmly hand in hand—the smell of granite and the wind from the Other World.

On some of the lower mountains I didn't feel the least bit connected to anything beyond the earth on which I stood, but now that the air was getting thin, and the climbs were above the clouds, my lungs ached with the reality that I was inhaling something from beyond. A mystical experience enveloped me at the top of these high climbs. When we yelled and waved at the sky after reaching the summit I could tell I was awakening a sleeping part of my soul. I could tell someone was listening as well—someone who was still higher than the place where I stood and the thin air was thick with His presence. It felt like some kind of supernatural approval. Like the smile on your mother's face when you do that thing—the thing you've been trying so hard to do—and without any words, with only the look, you feel completely, perfectly celebrated.

The local paper featured the beginning of my greatest climbing pursuit on the thirteenth page of the religion section—two bad omens. The *ValleyDweller Press* was not known for celebrating such "irrelevant" pursuits, and its predictable commitment to the party line of unbelief took no wind from my sails that day. That was the day I had marked on the calendar many months before with a tiny drawing of a mountain. I had marked off all the days prior, one day at a time, like a kid before Christmas. And when it arrived I was ready. Most people—definitely most of the press—had long died to any passion for the experience of the Mountain, and I knew it was a fool's game to look for approval from the satisfied masses in low altitude. I had fully assessed the consequences and the potential reward for myself, and when I made my decision, I made it in front of the skeptic, the supporter, the curious, and the neighbor across the street with no need of endorsement.

I set my face toward the work. I drove off with Chris, my gear, and my dream for the summit, and I vowed not to return until I reached my goal. I had already given up my old life, and without this experience I couldn't have a new one. My new life would be birthed on the summit and would go on in my living memory. I would touch the face of God, and having been changed by it I would not be a wandering dreamer any longer, but a living character in the Legend. Avoiding death was a given, but I was at peace with dying on the way, for at least my life would be spent well. If I died at the summit with God's face in my hands, so be it, I would have died fulfilled. If I fell to my death on the return, there would be no reason for tears because I would have stumbled while walking in the dream of my experience. If no one else could understand or celebrate my pursuit, so be it—there is nothing to be gained by the criticism of the uninitiated. I would become a taleteller that day, unable to return to my inferior life on the wheel.

Driving to base camp was a long, sweet good-bye.

It was the fortieth day of the climbing expedition, and it was destined to be the highest. Acclimation to the altitude is one of the most serious, and often overlooked, disciplines of climbing. Altitude forces a pace the climber must submit to, and in our case we had submitted to weeks of climbing and camping and waiting. To rush to the top is a rush to death with fluid filling the bursting lungs. We had listened to our bodies and the wisdom of other climbers, and the weather had allowed a good pace.

The sharp wind whistled over the ridge trying to bite our faces, and we fought to ignore it and focus on the inches we demanded from the last steep vertical face. The summit was in sight.

Chris and I had left the others at the high camp and made our attempt at the peak. We depended on each other, and we worked together, tying, pulling, anchoring, testing, breathing, ascending. The challenge was more than I had ever imagined. It was beyond my ability to prepare for, and the final stage was a different kind of test. My body rebelled against my plans, my mind disagreed with the pursuit, and I was left digging into some other reservoir of determination. It was deeper than the will or the intellect or the passion. It was a foolish courage with no need to be justified.

In retrospect, I wonder if what I found was *faith*?

Just feet from the top Chris asked me to move ahead, we adjusted our roles, and before I understood what was happening she said, "You have to go the rest alone." Was she out of her mind? I glanced toward the summit and realized what was before me. A slim channel ran directly before us to the tiny platform at the peak. From our route of ascent there was no other way, and there was room for only one climber at a time. One climber goes to the Summit, returns to this same vestibule, and then his partner can do the same. It was my time.

I pressed my hands and feet into the crevices and moved cautiously. It was a short distance, but it took what seemed like a day. There was not enough breath in me now to speak an audible word to my partner, who was slowly fading below the granite behind me. Just as I was about to stretch my hands toward what I thought was the rim of the summit, the unexplainable happened. A sharp pain shot through my body from hand to spine, my legs went soft, and I was left stunned, pressed to the side of the mountain. One hand stretched toward the top and one hand was in a deep crevice underneath me. I couldn't move anything at all, and for a moment I was lost. I had reached my vertical limit—my hard ceiling for living and climbing at the same time. The pain was my body's response to slamming into this ceiling, and it commanded to be relieved of duty. I was out, it was over, and I was dead to the summit.

I can't say now whether I whispered my prayer before or after I felt the hand wrapping around my wrist. I can't say now whether the voice I heard, the one that encouraged me to pray for help, came from outside or inside my head. I was deeply aware that both the voice and the hand were warm and strong. I knew the hand reached from above me, from the Summit platform, and began to pull me up. I did not protest for I knew my goal would have been completely lost without the rescue. I loved the rescue—what else would I have done? I loved the feeling of being drawn up toward the object of my affection, and I loved the sense that the answer to my whispered prayer was embodied so powerfully and so quickly in the hands of my quiet rescuer.

In a moment I saw and felt and tasted and heard and smelled everything from the Legend, all pressed together in the singular fulfillment of my dreams. I was kneeling on the Summit, the altar to the living God to my left, the figure of my Rescuer to my right (His hand now on my shoulder), and an endless horizon sweeping wide and beautiful in all directions. There was dancing and singing, weeping and silence. The Rescuer spoke eternity into my ear, but in return I could only whisper the word, "Yes."

In the epic moment I was pressed through a doorway of experience and with hands barely extended...I found myself...holding...the face...of God.

I found my head to be resting in His own hands as well, and soon I realized that love songs and Living Words were flowing out of His mouth and pouring over my face.

In the divine embrace all the questions of my heart were answered. I felt the peace that my chaos had been begging for. I was transported from the futile wheel of my past, and I knew I would never return to it again.

I was new.

Overcoming death has a way with a person's heart. It puts some recklessly happy thing in the driver's seat. Touching the face of God changes a person's whole being, and it gives the driver an understanding of the journey's end. For me, both were accomplished by an unseen Rescuer who came to me at the point of my absolute limit and with an approving touch erased my old life. He now walks with me in the new.

I live with a clear understanding of my debt, and I have been given the freedom to repay it with thankfulness. I am a Teller of the Tale now. I live the Legend. This is the way with all those having reached the Summit and returned to the valley. The air is clear all around me, and the horizon line is forever higher and wider. My name was rendered a very special thing in the mouth of God, and by decree it was written permanently into the pages of the Book. My deep and lasting joy, however, is not that my name was written down, but that I have held the warm, rescuing hand of the One who wrote it.

The Inner Realm

Finding God Thoughts

An online chat room is one thing; a face-to-face talk is another.

Having sex is one thing; living in a meaningful marriage is another.

Knowing about God is one thing; knowing God is another.

I am continually amazed at the number of religious people who want to reduce a meaningful relationship with God to a page of written principles. Have you met these people? They want to tell us that to know God we have to do this, don't do that, go here, don't go there, and then say a certain thing in a prayer, and *poof* we're "in." My question is, "in" to what? If I were on a personal quest to connect with God, why would I settle for a list of activities as a substitute?

I am equally unsatisfied with the common irreligious position that God is just "out there" somewhere, we should live the best we can, and we should relate to Him as we see fit. What? If the God of creation could be satisfied with just being "out there," then what hope is there for us? What is life if the originator of it is indifferent toward the living? If He places no parameters on our relationship then maybe He is dead.

Better dead than indifferent.

Imagine a marriage where the couple was counseled in homemaking, financial planning, child raising, and monogamy, but were never encouraged to speak to one another. Sounds fun, doesn't it? People who know about each other or acknowledge each other's existence are not in relationship. Two people living in the same house are not married. Two people who agree to respect each other and share resources are not really intimate. This marriage picture illustrates the difference between the form—the "outside" of a relationship, and the true nature of an *intimate* relationship. Intimacy requires so much vulnerability, honesty, commitment, risk, and trust. The potential reward is romance, adventure, and an exciting life! Could this really be possible with God?

Before we flinch at the "God wants a marriage" analogy we should note that in the ancient writings of the prophet Hosea God makes that very claim. He says, "In that day you will call me your Husband, not your Master." If nothing else, this kind of language begs us to consider what we really want from God. Do we want to be roommates, sharing the furniture but not our lives? Do we want to wear His nametag in public, but not love Him in private?

I doubt any of us would want a marriage partner who lived in our home, used our money, and raised our children, but didn't care for us at all. In the same way we should refuse to identify with religion that requires the same pathetic arrangements and calls it "relationship with God." We should also refuse any notion that God can be held at a distance and would accept some anonymous role in our lives. Any caring, committed marriage has rules and boundaries, but those rules do not stir the heart to beat faster or cause the face to blush. I will abide by the rules after I have found the object of my affection. After my heart has been captured I will commit myself willingly to the boundaries of honor and respect with the God that proves His relentless love for me— and brings some real life and adventure to my world!

If knowing God is experiential, why shouldn't we *enjoy the experience?*

What is God if He is not enjoyable?

The Barista Knows

Java Boy

Finishing grad school was a relief. I missed my family. I loved my friends, but I missed my family. I left the great, green Northwest for the dry mountains of Colorado to attend school, and now I wasn't quite sure what to do. I had finished one thing that I set out to do, but some things were left undone.

The cross-country trek to the Rockies had been filled with great sights and sounds. My car stereo was happy to burn in most of the new music I picked up at the CD-Xchange trading shop.

I stood staring at my CD collection for a long time before I could decide what to purge. It was like standing in front of the closet trying to decide which articles to donate to Goodwill. I gritted my teeth and I ruthlessly purged. The trade got me into some Euro-Techno stuff, some obscure club bands, a couple of new ethnic instrumentals, and a disc by a singer-songwriter I had heard of, but never listened to.

I also had no idea how scarce decent coffeehouses were in America. The drive turned into one big coffee safari. Mile after mile I drove on, using the search for good espresso as an excuse to get off the highway. Then I would blow off the whole town and drive on if no good coffee was found. Oh, sure, something like coffee was available at all of these stops: round pots sitting on warmers with cardboard-flavored dirt water in them. If you drank it fast it would burn the taste buds off your tongue (I assumed that was the point). For the sake of ingesting caffeine, many people drank the stuff without giving any thought to the intestinal meltdown that would soon follow. This coffee-lax beverage is the primary reason, in my opinion, that truckers drive too fast and roadside restrooms are always filthy. Some stores had the audacity to put the neon word "Cappuccino" in the front window. The neon should have read "Hot beverage made from powdery space age polymers that tastes like old milk and bad candy in a blender." It squirted out of a tube into a paper cup and took the money of deluded travelers. The regular coffee-lax customers viewed it as a beverage for sophisticates. I viewed it as a personal attack.

It was on the last half of the long relocation that I began to reconsider God.

I dated girls who believed in God, I went to a few religious services, but I spent little time on the subject myself. On a long stretch between gas stations I started talking out loud to myself, and then to God, and then to my car, and then to God again. It was a perfect time to have an open question-and-answer session. I was an adult, I was not under the influence of any mind-altering religious pressure, and I was curious.

I had a lot of questions.

I had a few complaints.

If God was out there, would He care to listen?

My undergrad philosophy classes and my one comparative religion class had primed the pump, but they had offered no real answers to the questions plaguing my mind. As I pulled into the artsy little university town in central Colorado, I turned off the CD player, threw one of the stupid Euro-beat music CDs into the back seat, and closed my long dialogue with God. It went something like this:

"I want to know what You are really like. I want to make some kind of decision about religion and my future before I leave school this year. Help me, God, if You are out there, to know what to do."

Here I am sitting at this little coffee bar three years later having a private graduation celebration. My family would be coming in this weekend for the ceremonies and a whole lot of backslapping, but I didn't feel like I was quite finished. I didn't feel quite *satisfied*. I had made very little progress in my own spiritual life, and it was still bothering me. I had scored high in my class, completed a great thesis, and enjoyed a semester abroad on a cultural exchange in India. But I had not yet answered some of my deeper questions. I knew there was more to the spiritual than I had seen, but where would I look?

I leaned over the bar toward the now familiar barista and asked, "I've been trying to figure out this bizarre art on the back wall for months now."

"You're not the only one."

"Is the artist from around here?"

"Yeah. The owner knows her. Her card is on the board in the back. It says 'worship...*something*...'" His words trailed off under the grinder's noise.

I went back into the little hall and found, underneath a pile of concert posters and "For Sale" ads, a single business card that read:

In Ritual

Every day, very early in the day, I tend to my tiny garden. It reminds me of the simplicity and order of life. The way I draw my rake over the tiny white rocks moves them around the little box and creates fine, even patterns. I feel sometimes that the action is a cross between petting a cat and washing my hands compulsively, but it gives me a sense of order so I do it—every day.

Forgetting oneself is a full-time job. I wonder how anyone could ever do it, but in keeping with the teaching I do not allow that "wonder" to become a doubt in the truthfulness of the teaching.

My stereo system is covered with dust from the incense burner. The running joke is that if I ever clean it, it will never work again. I put on my favorite recording of rainforest sounds mixed with some flute-like instruments, kneel, and open the doors of my little altar. My meditation today is focused on being happy. Something from the Dalai Lama I think. "Be happy, smile, smile, be happy, why not be happy, pretending to be happy is better than pretending to be sad, we are all pretending anyway, be happy, smile, smile, smile" or something like that. It doesn't really matter what I say, because the teachings prohibit fixation on formulas or creeds. I like that. I feel better after I meditate most days.

Closing the tiny doors and placing my incense in the holder, I go on with my morning routine. Soon my mind wanders to the issue with my family, the trouble with my new boss, and the nagging feeling that I am missing something in the teachings—something around the corner, hidden under a precept, that is prohibiting me from attaining my new nature. I would try harder. Or maybe I should not "try" at all. Either way I will find the answer.

If life were like a tiny garden with clean white rocks it would be so much easier.

Most of my feelings of vulnerability leave by the time I pack my vegetarian lunch. I am in control of some things. Pressing the ends of the incense into a little tray to extinguish them, I grab my keys from the hook and head out the door. The unruly world meets me with honking and shoving, and no matter where I turn there are no smiles on any of the faces.

If they only knew.

Through Art

God touches us through art.

The mathematician is consigned to numbers. The biologist is restricted to organic matter. The philosopher uses only words. The artist, on the other hand, is unrestricted in expression. The only limits are self-imposed.

The picture that is worth a thousand words might also contain a hundred insights. The sculpture that represents only one natural figure might also represent a score of supernatural truths. The film, held on one reel, might reveal dozens of secrets about the world around us. The four-minute song might contain a lifetime's worth of revelation about life and love. The moving narrative on the pages of a single book might open up a brand-new landscape of meaning to us.

God chooses the artistic handiwork of people to reveal Himself to us. This touch does not come through the artistic agent like a bad photocopy of an original work. True artists never simply retell the obvious or state the physical facts. True artists tell the story of what they have seen and experienced. Some of the insights start with the natural, and some start with the Other World. The tangible world, and all that is in it, becomes part of the artist's language, but their stories are not limited to the substance of their language. Sometimes they tell the story of God.

One might argue that since not all artists believe in God, we could not find Him in their work. On the contrary, many artists who do believe in God have so poorly caricatured His nature that the cartoons they relay do little but diminish Him. It is often the innocent and the uninitiated that give best expression to a vision of God. Some artistic visions are birthed in protest to the divine, and some are birthed in cooperation, but either way God can often be found reaching out from the work. Whether in realism or wild abstraction, the artist has the ability to tell the story of experience, and we have the opportunity to listen for the Divine.

This Path of Seven is a guided tour through human creativity that might reveal more of the pursuing presence of God than we might expect.

1. Go see a movie. Save money by going to a matinee. Before the previews start, whisper, "God, I want to see You in this movie. Show me where You are in it, and show me what You are like through it." Discuss your insights with a friend or with yourself after the show.

2. Visit a local art gallery when you have a few minutes to stay. Cruise your chosen part of the exhibit with your normal routine. Read the cards and pick your favorite. Now sit down where you can be still. Ask God, "What part of You is revealed in this art?" Wait. Write it down. For a bonus, ask God, "What part of You is revealed in the artist?" Wait. Write it down.

3. Have a Renaissance moment. Pull down the art appreciation book or do a Web search and find some classic Renaissance work (like Michelangelo, DaVinci, or Rembrandt), and ask God, "What did You like about the way these artists represented You?" Wait. Write it down like an art critic who is interviewing God.

4. Put on your favorite CD. Lie on the floor near the speakers, and before you press "Play," say out loud, "I want to hear the voice of God in this music. I want to sense Him reaching out

to me." As soon as you get an insight stop the music and write it down. Was God in the words of the singer? Was He speaking through the rhythm? Was He answering the lyrics from outside the performance?

5. Find a sculpture you can touch. It could be a figurine in your house or a large interactive piece in the park. Close your eyes and run your hands over the work. What was it like to create this piece? How did the dream come? What was it like to create the world? How did the dream come?

6. Read a classic short story. Before you begin insert a small piece of paper in the back and keep a pen handy for taking notes. Ask these questions as you read, and write down what you find. "Are their any worshipers in this story, and, if so, what are they worshiping?" "Who is running from God in this story?" "How does this story make me feel about relating to God?"

7. Find some modern art. Look over the collection with your physical eyes: notice color, line, shape, and energy. Now ask, "God, give me spiritual eyes." You may have a deeper sense about the work. Is there anger or celebration? Is there order or chaos in the heart? If God were sitting next to you what do you think He would see?

Thoughts
Preparing To Enter

Strange idea, isn't it? That every molecule, every working cell of our body, is the direct result of the imagination of God?

It's a strange miracle.

I admit that I do like this idea better than believing that every molecule of my body is the indirect result of billions of years of cosmic accidents that fell together to create a living entity with will, emotion, love, dreams, and the desire to worship an Eternal Being. I have decided which choice takes greater faith. I have decided which creates a more exciting and valuable life.

In this process of choosing I discovered there are some non-negotiable adjustments that we have to make in our posture to make room for God. We have to change our attitude to fit our worldview. After all, if our actions don't match our beliefs, then the whole package should be called into question.

Our actions always give voice to our beliefs. Our actions will prove what we believe about God and ourselves. This simple truth can help us discern false religion from true religion. It can help us discern false people from true people, and find out where we fall in the mix. We may find both proof and inconsistency in our own lives.

The first part of most people's search into the nature of God probably begins with questions about the nature of our own life.

Where did we come from?

What is the *origin of the species*?

Any true belief in God must deal clearly and adequately with the question of our origin. It is not enough to speak about the future, about eternity, about extraterrestrial life, or about the apocalypse—we must also converse about a meaningful beginning. We are meaningful beings and we need to know why. Answers like "We're just here," "Being is relative," or "Existence is a state of mind" are all bizarre and inadequate answers. What these things say to us is that our past is not real, our present is irrelevant, and our future is inconsequential. Useless.

Many religious people like to answer the question of origin with a simple bumper sticker reading "Creationism," but they spend no time trying to understand what "Creation" really means. They are dishonest in their claim to believe in creation, because they fail to demonstrate the direct result of being created—humility. Pride has given them away.

Ever wonder what kind of pride could evolve from being created?

The created person has no ownership of the copyright on the invention of life. They have no insight into the actual work of their beginnings because they were not witnesses to it. The "created" are a walking testimony of the genius of the creator but have no claim to the power of their inception. It is no wonder that people who crave independence avoid the idea of being created—it demands absolute humility and dependence. People who claim to know God and believe in creation, but choose to be independent as well, are living out the worst of contradictions. They give new definition to the word hypocrite when they try to mix pride and creationism. I am not sure which is worse: the rebellious or the hypocrite.

Want a test to find out if people really believe that God created them?

Look for signs of humility.

See if they love others who disagree with them. See if they bless their enemies, or if they want to purge the earth of them. Find out if they are driven to defend the "rightness" of their position, or if they can be silent when slandered. Find out if they take credit for the good in their life, or if they seem always to give the credit away. Do they fixate on themselves and their practice, or on God and His presence? To associate with the humble is a great step toward understanding God.

An ancient saying declares, "God opposes the proud, but gives grace to the humble." This sounds true to the nature of things, doesn't it? As we realize that a true God must be a creating God, and that we are all a result of His work, we are led to a very specific choice. This choice is a prerequisite for approaching God and getting to know Him better, and it is made by people who stop and take a long hard look at the inside of their own heart.

We have to choose to be humble...and from the look of things, we may need some serious help.

The Center

Curious Things

Vision

When I was first taken up into the vision I never quite lost the feel of the floor underneath my back. My hands rested quietly on my skirt spread loosely around me, and my eyes closed to discover an unfolding scene where I was standing center.

The walls collapsed. The furnishings were swept out and away. The sound of the music was there, but not nearly as close as it was before.

I was surrounded by thousands of people, but none of them had faces, and it didn't matter. What mattered was the way they all moved about in odd little circles and back and forth. Looking at their hands. Looking at their feet. Making short, suspicious glances toward one another. The jittering movement never stopped, and a dull mumbling sound swirled around me on all sides as they moved past me, around me, back and forth. Everyone was very busy in this strange, useless exercise, and the awkwardness of it made me feel sick.

In my desire to move away I was immediately turned to a point of illumination that could have been on the horizon. It was not the horizon, however, because there was no floor, no ceiling, no landscape, no sun. We were all on the same horizontal plane but we were not walking, and it was not dark but the place in the distance was definitely glowing with its own kind of light.

I moved toward the glowing area, and coming closer, I noticed two distinct things. The movement in this new area was different from the movement of the hectic people around me. There was a slow rhythm in it. Just as I noticed the subtle rhythm I realized there was singing. There were many voices and one distinct, warm voice.

Did I hear my name?

The thought arrested my heart and I pushed as hard as I could toward the...circle? It was a circle, broad and flat.

I could see people surrounding the circle on every side. Some were pointing and laughing, some were yelling and taunting, some stood deadpan, staring, and all the while the people inside the circle paid them no mind. The circle was filled with people of all shapes and sizes, young and old. Some were sitting, some were standing, and some were lying down. As I worked to push through the crowd, I began to see more figures and more activity in the circle. I got the strange impression that something in the center of the great ring was generating all the interest. The music and the heavy sounds and the warm voice seemed to be coming from the middle of everything.

Was that my name again?

The Inhabitants

Thoughts

At this point in our journey Jesus Christ must be seriously considered.

Why?

Jesus Christ has unlocked the door into the mysteries of worship, eternity, and meaning for me, and it is my journey that I am relaying. I am not treating other religious systems or leaders here because they have not entered my personal story with similar impact. Yes, it is my opinion, my experience, but please resist the urge to close the book to avoid hearing a sermon from another Christian. I am not sure that I am a "Christian" in today's terms. We all know that the term "Christian" can cover a great variety of human experience and effort, both good and bad. The word can mean something ethnic, something national, something philosophical, and something spiritual. It vibrates with reactions because so many saints and tyrants, homophobes and heroes, pedophiles and preachers have worn it on their lapels. Let's discard it from our conversation because *Christian* is both a volatile and misused word in the modern world.

I can't say that I have found the perfect, single word to describe my spiritual journey. There are terms like "believer" and "disciple," but I am not sure if they would fully describe my world. The term "Follower of the Way" was used shortly after Jesus' life to refer to the sect of people who were given to His teachings and lived according to His claims. I think we can examine these people and what the term meant to their world in order to better understand my present experience.

One of the most notable believers in these early years was a man named Paul, but he did not rise to fame as a believer—quite the contrary. He was leading the war of hate waged directly at the Followers of the Way and the Jesus they believed in. He was a very religious man who hated the fact that this sect defied the religious "right" of the time. His obsession with religious things grew into a deep bigotry. He was a perfect stereotype of the prideful religious zealot, and though they don't all follow through with the same intensity, they do all think the same.

His infamy is recounted in the Book of Acts, which is mostly an overview of the beginnings of the Way. In this book we find Paul standing by and giving approval as his fellow zealots crushed the skull of a young Follower of the Way with stones—hurled with murderous insult and religious pride. These prejudiced persecutors belonged to a superior race, an elite club of thought and spiritual practice. Those who challenged Paul's point of view were not worthy of the privilege of life, and he would rather have killed them than continue to hear their absurd beliefs. He even sought special permission to visit other cities infested with the Way "so that if he found any there who belonged to the Way, whether men or women, he might take them as prisoners." Different beliefs are an intolerable plague and a distraction for those who possess this kind of arrogant "truth." He was perfectly religious and perfectly ruthless.

Nothing has changed for close-minded religious zealots in the modern world. They simply wear different hats: clergy, journalist, professor, philosopher, or politician.

Everything changed in the heart of Paul.

Paul had an encounter with Jesus Christ. It changed his life. It redefined his entire existence. It confounded the other zealots and stunned the Followers of the Way. His unbelievable transformation and his subsequent commitment to following Jesus fill most of the early accounts of the growth of the Way in the ancient world. His story sets the stage for us to better understand them...and me.

If we discover what makes the Followers unique then we will better understand Christ's own claims and the opportunity ahead of us. I believe we will discover the Followers of the Way engaging a God who is truly *worthy* of our worship.

First we should note their *initiation*.

Follower of the Way, as it is used in these early writings, may apply to people of any color, any race, and any socioeconomic background who have had an encounter with Jesus Christ.

It still does today.

I could not become a Follower of the Way until I had met the central figure. I could not claim the title of "Follower" until I had first been personally arrested by His presence—not just His teachings.

Paul's *initiation* took place on one of his "seek and destroy" missions. He encountered the supernatural presence of Christ when he least expected to encounter anything at all, and he was changed—not by an idea, but by the supernatural reality of God:

> As he neared Damascus on his journey, suddenly a light from heaven flashed around him. He fell to the ground and heard a voice say to him, "Saul, Saul, why do you persecute me?"
>
> "Who are you, Lord?" Saul asked.
>
> "I am Jesus, whom you are persecuting," he replied. "Now get up and go into the city, and you will be told what you must do." The men traveling with Saul stood there speechless; they heard

the sound but did not see anyone.

Now Paul (also called Saul) had regarded the Followers of the Way as individual enemies, but when he met Christ he discovered there was only one enemy. Christ spoke to him and said, "I am Jesus, whom you are persecuting."

Strange?

Not really.

Paul knew immediately that he was not really fighting individuals. He was fighting an unseen force that gnawed at his spirit and made him uncomfortable with himself. So uncomfortable, so uneasy was his life, that he was driven to destroy the cause of his annoyance. This trouble was embodied in the Followers of the Way, and by breaking them down he was hoping to get some relief. Suddenly, the One whom these Followers had embodied, the One whom he was out to destroy, was speaking to him.

Undeniably real.

Undeniably supernatural.

I have, like many others, mistakenly attributed the annoying power of the Followers of the Way to something they individually possessed. Many have sought to shield themselves from this annoyance by ridiculing the Followers, exposing their weaknesses, challenging their legitimacy, and even destroying them. But the thing that truly annoys us is *beyond* the Followers, and Paul met *Him*—face to face.

My encounter was not quite as dramatic, but the ingredients were the same. I was pursuing my own agenda when Christ interrupted me. He caught my attention. He stopped my selfish progress. I was a young man when I looked into the gathering of Followers and felt that deep annoyance. Something was missing. I could feel God gnawing at my life, and I knew when the speaker quoted that Bible passage—"For God so loved the world..." that God had a demanding love for me. There was a deep cry in my heart, and His hands were wrapped around it. I wanted to touch the face of God, and Jesus was bringing Him near.

Never let anyone reduce Following the Way to a pathetic list of religious ideas. No idea will transform a living being. It is not *the idea* of gravity that forces us to the ground, and it is not *the idea* of God that challenges our hearts so relentlessly. Some things are real because *they are real*. We encounter them and prove them so.

How do I know?

Well, my understanding is based on more than blind faith, but I do confess that I began my journey closer to blindness than to anything else. Like the woman who meets the man of her dreams and knows he is "the one" before they ever go on a date, I was first initiated into God, and then I spent the years following discovering why He so deserved my heart. I did not climb the ladder of scientific proof onto the lap of God, but once I had met Him I went on to find not only the ladder of science, but also the ladders of nature, art, romance, and experience that lead to Him as well.

It is also absurd to equate the Way with a religion where the rules of conduct define its membership. Listing good things and bad things can categorize the world, but it cannot introduce a person to God. Blueprints and formulas do not serve our free nature very well. Have you ever tried to put a large cat in a small box? Our spirit is a wild, living thing, and it cannot be brought into conformity by external forces like a hand pressing unwilling clay. These external forces will only cause us harm. What we need is a supernatural encounter that transforms us in a different way...from the inside out.

No pre-existent condition can guarantee someone's membership in the Way. We cannot be born into the Way, or taught into the

Way, or bought into the Way. Every person who begins this journey is initiated through a supernatural experience with Jesus Christ. To give us insight He once said, "I tell you the truth, anyone who will not receive the kingdom of God like a little child will never enter it," and then to demonstrate better what that looked like He "took the children in his arms, put his hands on them and blessed them." It is not important to wrestle with the concept of the "kingdom of God," but it is important to notice how Jesus Christ personally touched the little children to demonstrate what our entrance into a relationship with Him would be like.

The God of the Way is intensely personal, and He refuses to be pushed away into the outfield of the cosmos. Do you want to meet Him?

In Children

The dirt is cooling under my feet as we make our way to the meeting. My favorite time of the day is when the sky turns colors, the dirt in the street cools, and all my family is home from the fields and the work of the day. My short legs strain to keep up with my father and older brother, who always seem to set the pace. I know they won't leave me.

It has been seven years since the men came from the neighboring village with the message of God's love. I can't remember when they came; I was too young. But my older brother says they brought new seeds for planting and new things to keep the water clean, and that is why we are living in a very happy time now. My father always says, "It is the *good Lord* we will thank, not the *good seeds*."

Tonight as we come over the rise in the road I can see the lights strung around the edge of the open building. The beams holding the roof are like black lines in front of all the people inside, who are singing and clapping. The electric lights dance with the music like they are worshiping too. I can feel the drone of the generator. My whole family starts to sing along as we walk toward the big meeting.

There is always a lot of dancing and shouting and tambourine shaking at these meetings. Someone is already screaming and thrashing around at the front, and the leaders are going to pray for her and send the evil spirit away. We don't believe in witchcraft anymore, but we do believe in the evil spirits. Mostly, we believe in Jesus.

Tonight I was singing and smiling, with all my heart I was happy. Soon I would be old enough, father said, to be baptized into the church. I had already told them I wanted to be baptized. I told them I loved Jesus, too, and when my brother was baptized my mother had to hold me so I wouldn't run into the river! When Jesus healed my mother from the fever, and healed the screaming people at the meetings, and made our whole family so happy, how could I not love Him? I learned the Scriptures like the other children in my school, and I loved to say them out loud: "For God so loved the world that he gave his one and only Son, that whoever believes in him shall not perish but have eternal life."

The screaming woman is still lying limp on the floor (not screaming anymore) as we all dance up to the front to give our offerings to God. Father told me I could worship God by giving some of the money I had saved to help the other Christians and to help the poor. Tonight, as I stretch toward the box on the table, I still can't reach the opening in the top, so I just press the coin onto the tabletop. I feel very good.

The preacher speaks about many things, but mostly the love of Jesus. Now, however, he is speaking about the promise of the Holy Spirit. My heart is beating so fast. I know that I want the Holy Spirit to live in me just like the preacher is saying. Without telling anyone I close my eyes and I pray. I can still hear the preacher and still feel my mother rocking back and forth on the wooden bench. "Dear God, I believe in Jesus. I believe in Your cross, and I love You too. Will You give me Your Holy Spirit tonight?"

No more amazing thing has ever visited a little boy.

The Connection

Thoughts

Not only is Christ the *initiation* into the Way, but He is also the intimate partner along the journey that we continue. As we move on to look deeper into these things, a couple of questions may prick at our minds. The first question might be, "Why did Jesus call Paul 'Saul' during the encounter on the road to Damascus?"

Saul was Paul's Jewish name. It originated in his Hebrew tradition, and he used it to identify with the religious, Hebrew world. He was born, however, in the Roman city of Tarsus and was by birth a Roman citizen. In a bilingual world (Hebrew and Greek) he used the Greek name, Paul, to identify with the rest of the Roman Empire, and because the bulk of his recorded life was lived out in that world that is how we have commonly known him.

Jesus, however, begins His address by appealing to Paul's core identity as a man of *religious* culture. Paul's spiritual equations are all built inside of his Hebrew identity, and Jesus meets Paul where he is most ready to have conversation—in the context of his religious zeal.

Saul.

The subtle but important message here is that Jesus begins His conversation with us right where we are living. If we are living in a religious equation, He will begin there. If we are living in an atheistic formula, He will begin there. If we find ourselves held deep inside our cultural identity, He will begin there.

Why?

Because *He wants to connect.*

To have a real conversation with someone we adjust our language to fit the relationship. If we speak with an elder, we adjust our language and posture to fit. If we speak with a marriage partner we adjust, if we speak with a child we adjust—because we *want to connect.* If we don't want to connect with someone we naturally refuse to adjust our language, for instance: when we refuse to use terms of respect for the elder, we remove the terms of endearment toward our romantic partner, or when we speak "over the heads" of younger people. Christ did not do this to Paul—He leaned way over and spoke a personal word of connection.

Saul.

Christ wanted to connect! The God of the Way is pursuing us! He did not just want to shock Paul into submission and amaze him with a bright light and a thunderclap. Jesus Christ desperately wants to connect with us, and that is why He can, and He will, adjust His language for us. How do you think He should speak to you?

Many religions are home to prophets, teachers, and transformed beings who have touched the "divine" and brought back a system of belief for their followers. Many religions (including much of modern Christian traditions) have gods that run the universe, issue rules for living, but never personally reach out and care for a single human being.

How unsatisfactory.

Jesus is best understood as the living gesture of God, leaning way over to press His love for humanity right into our view. And He apparently desires to connect with us even when we don't want to connect with Him!

Paul may have begun his connection with Jesus on the road to Damascus, but the conversation did not end there. This is the second defining element in our discovery: Followers of the Way are living an ongoing connection with the divine. Some may say that their religious tradition contains supernatural encounters, but Followers of the Way continuously live in a connection to the supernatural. Some belong to religions where their spiritual leaders have had divine encounters, but they themselves have not. Some visit sacred places where the divine once visited as well. I have heard countless people say, "I had a spiritual experience back in such-and-such time," and they can tell the story of the past event, but they are at a loss for words when describing their spiritual present. The true Followers of the Way are easy to pick out because they are telling the story of a continuing experience with the divine. Jesus promised this ongoing relationship when He said, simply, "Remain in me, and I will remain in you."

For those of us who are not willing to settle for someone else's experience, or someone else's truth, Jesus Christ holds the claim and the key to a lasting connection with God.

The Goal

Jesus said, "I am the gate; whoever enters through me will be saved. He will come in and go out, and find pasture. The thief comes only to steal and kill and destroy; I have come that they may have life, and have it to the full."

So what did He mean when He said, "I am the *gate*," and what in the world is being *saved*?

A gate is a point of entry or exit. "The," in His statement, implies that there is no other gate like the one He is referencing. Why? First of all, Jesus Christ represents the God first introduced in the history of Hebrew experience. This God was always asking the same question:

"Will you love Me?"

The ancient Hebrews didn't hear the question clearly, and neither do we. Fear, pride, lack of trust, misconceptions of God, and self-ishness clogged their hearing. Reading the Old Testament of the Bible (the first half) is like reading a soap opera script where the pursuing lover (God) and unwilling bride (the Hebrews) never quite connect. The whole Old Testament writing titled "Hosea" is dedicated to describing this romantic dilemma. They constantly proved their inability to love Him in return. By the time Jesus enters history, the Hebrews had so deluded themselves that they had no idea what He was saying when He told them, "You diligently study the Scriptures because you think that by them you possess eternal life. These are the Scriptures that testify about me, yet you refuse to come to me to have life."

God still comes wanting to connect with us personally, but we opt for many things as a substitute and many activities as a diversion. The God of the Way refuses to relate to us from a distance, however, and Christ goes on to prove that fact. He will not send us a book and be satisfied with having "readers." He will not send us some rituals and be satisfied with "practitioners." He is looking for something much deeper, much more personal, and so He visits us in an intensely personal way.

God is still asking the question, "Do you love Me?"

In response to our inability to understand the question, God does something radical in the person of Jesus Christ. In the drama that shapes the Follower of the Way's understanding of history, the God who talked with Moses, spoke with David, and dealt with Jonah *decided to come to earth* and do away with the misconceptions about His love for us.

He came in a human form of self-expression.

Being wonderfully creative, He wrote a song, a play, a poem, and an epic love story—all wrapped up in the life of His Son, Jesus Christ.

He is God's "Son," because the best expression of a father's creative power is in the life of his son. "Son," because He could represent His Father in a finite world without reducing the infinite nature of His Dad. "Son," so that when He hung, dying on the cross, it would be clear that it was a family matter, and "no" would never be an acceptable answer. Jesus Christ lived and died and was resurrected from the dead for one purpose: to demonstrate the love God has for all of us. His selfless act of love would remove any suspicions that God did not truly love us. The life and death of Christ both ask the question, "Do you love Me?"

Followers of the Way hear Christ calling us to join hands with the God of pursuing love. If we reach to take His hands, however, we will find that they have nail scars from His death on the cross. What does this mean? For Followers of the Way, the cross is far beyond a piece of religious jewelry. It is not a power icon.

It is a humbling reminder.

The cross tells two important stories. It first tells the story of God's romantic pursuit of humanity and the tragic moment we rejected His advances by nailing Him to the tree. This speaks of His unconditional love. Secondly, it tells the story of a rescuing act that is powerful enough to bridge the gap between us and the God we desperately need.

God pursues us across history, against all odds and against our own wishes, to pour His love out on us. God throws Himself in front of the train called "Independence" and stops our death wish in its tracks. The cross demonstrates that God was willing to assume the lowest position of human rejection, a death reserved for the worst criminals of the state, in order to woo the hearts of the accusers themselves. No one could ever say again, "God doesn't love me...God doesn't care...God may be real, but I can live

as I want and it will all be OK." The arresting picture of the God of Creation suffering under our own death wish has forever interrupted the flow of prophets and teachers and gurus who have come to show us the way—*Jesus Christ came to be the Way*.

Christ opens only one gate because according to His own life and mission, *He is the gate and there is only one of Him*. He invites us to connect to *the pursuing God*, and then He demonstrates on the cross just how passionately God pursues. Christ can't open other gates because the gate, the invitation, the journey, and the goal are all wrapped up in Him. Christ is all in all, both the question and the answer, to the Followers of the Way. To consider other gates may be necessary in our research, but to walk through them is to discover a different promise, a different god, and a different end result.

The ultimate goal then, the high pursuit for the Followers of the Way, is to be fully united with the God of Pursuing Love. The path of reunion is the life and death and resurrection of Christ. These Followers must not be confused with those who call themselves "Christians" and whose goal is be perfect, or to be spiritually wise, or to be *right*. The Followers are more interested in being *connected* than being perfect, and they trust Christ to make *the Way*.

When God asks the question, "Do you love me?", are you ready to form an answer?

Fury Of Love

I found myself in an open spot at the edge of the circle, and I looked toward the voice that had called my name. As my eyes scanned across the great ring I could see that the movement, the music, and the light intensified toward the center of the circle. It was from the center of the circle that I heard the warm voice.

What I saw next was beyond anything in my wildest imagination. The intensity of the vision was not contained in the image itself—many of my dreams have contained wild and complex images. The power of it lay on the other side of what I could see. Every facet of what I saw held a deep, piercing meaning, and this deep thing was touching something deep inside of me.

There were many things, but there was only one. I could see them all at once, and all at once more things were unfolding. Those I remember I will tell.

In the center stood a Being with one hand on a throne and one hand extended toward me. His eyes were like fire, not because they were aflame, but because my soul was on fire when He looked at me. His mouth moved, and words I couldn't understand flowed out, but I could feel them cutting my heart like a sword through my chest.

It was not the fear to run that I felt. It was the fear to stay.

This was not a man. It was at once a Lion, a Man, a Child, a King, and a Lamb. He was more than these, but these I can tell.

He was tattooed. One tattoo on His thigh I could read, but there was one in a language I couldn't read, and the names of millions were written on the palms of his hands. Colors and sounds and expressions poured out from Him into the circle of the gathered. Horses and armies rushed around and underneath Him, but none obscured our view. I saw old men and strange creatures that bowed and prayed. Each of the Great Being's movements unfolded a new facet of His wonder, and a wave of amazement swept through the creatures, the bowing men, the swirling armies, and the dancing and singing and weeping peoples. I sensed a fury of love and adoration here—so much joy that it spun everything round and round in a dizzying dance. I wanted to leap from where I was and be swept into it all, but as I leaned forward I found my feet were frozen fast in the concrete at the edge of the circle.

Just then, as though it was choreographed for the universe, the entire vision went soft and quiet. All the motion slowed and blurred. All except one. The Great Being was as clear to me as bright crystal held to the sun, and I saw His shoulders square toward me and both of His arms stretch out, His hands open.

If what I saw next was real…

The Changing Thoughts

So, just what is the idea of "salvation" or being "saved" that Jesus spoke of? According to the Way it might be more than one thing. It could be salvation from the striving of religious activity. It could be escape from the tired drone of a purposeless life. It could be salvation from the mouse-wheel of existence apart from God. But more than being salvation *from something*, it is mostly salvation *to something*—a deliverance into the presence of God.

Deliverance is a great word picture. It implies transportation, it promises a better place, and it demonstrates the action of a benevolent power. Followers of the Way are on a journey. I am on that journey. I have not reached a destination where I sit comfortably at a desk and issue invitations to the rest of the unbelieving world to join me in my state of perfection. I am traveling, and as I travel you may watch, you may join, or you may wave as I pass. Nonetheless, I am constantly being transported into the presence of God.

Followers of the Way are not wanderers because they are traveling toward a specific destination. The Followers' strange confession, however, is that they are not traveling under their own power. This is much different from the self-help versions of spiritual pursuit.

They are *being* delivered. They are *being* saved.

The goal? A singular high place—the presence of the living God. This is not a geographical place. This is not a stone temple, or a mosque, or a mountain. God doesn't have room for His feet in these manmade shrines or in the places He created with His fingertips. The Followers are encouraged to understand that "we are the temple of the Living God." As God has said through the prophets, "I will live with them and walk among them, and I will be their God, and they will be My people." As He lives inside of us He promises to transform us from the inside out, but the *changing* is not our goal—it is a by-product of the adventure.

The beauty of this reality is we are released from the obligation to change ourselves. We do not have to pretend to be someone better. We no longer have to find our own way to reach the face of God, or to forgive others, or to escape addiction, loneliness, or lack. The Spirit—the presence—of God enters the inner being of the Follower and begins to rebuild the heart from the inside out. The rebuilding, healing presence of God reshapes even our motives so we can live and love like we have always imagined. The only discipline the Follower has to commit himself to is the work of remaining in the presence of God and enjoying the relationship. God performs the transformation. No other religion, no other claimant, no other spiritual idea has ever come close to this unbelievable proposition. It was a promise spoken into the earth before Jesus walked on it. Four hundred years earlier God spoke to a prophet named Ezekiel who had been standing, in a vision, over a pile of dried human bones. The prophet knew the bones represented the hopeless, lifeless state of humanity. God spoke to Ezekiel about what He could do to the bones, to him, and to all of us when He said, "And I will put My Spirit in you and move you to follow My decrees...I will put My Spirit in you and you will live."

One thing certain about the Followers of the Way is that their lives are changing, and they are changing for the better. Have you ever wanted to change?

Micro-Roast

I had held the card in my wallet for only a few days. I turned to the calendar and realized it was Friday. Tomorrow my family would arrive for the graduation activities, but tonight I was free.

Passing several shops and galleries into the cultural district of the city, I walked with determination down Main Street. I had to be determined because I was a little nervous and thought that any moment, given almost any excuse, I would turn around and go home. The things that always made me feel a bit upside down were meeting girls, attending religious events, and walking into a room full of strangers. Tonight I would do all three.

The old Civic Theater was always in view, but was always passed by. No movies, no plays or concerts, had been promoted there for quite some time. I had thought, like most others, that it was simply the victim of poor management and the flight of money to the glossy entertainment of the suburbs. I thought it was cool that anything was going on in the building at all, and I used that hopeful expectation to get me through the front doors.

7:20 p.m.

I wondered if my watch was right.

I wondered if everyone was going to turn and stare at me when I walked in late.

I wondered who "everyone" might be.

Much to my relief, when I got into the vestibule of the theater and passed a few people loitering in the entry, I realized there was some kind of concert going on. I was glad for the noise—music is such a great cover for entering and exiting anywhere. People would be distracted, and that meant I could find my way in, check everything out, decide if I was going to stay or leave, and then improvise a plan. As I made my way to the theater entrance I was flanked by tables with snacks and flyers and books and…coffee! It was coffee in big vacuum pots, but they had the bags of whole beans out on the counter, and I recognized the name of the local roaster. I thought to myself, "Well, at least these people have gotten one thing right." I pushed open the door enough to see inside and was met with a myriad of activity.

Rather than describe the detail of activity I saw on that first night, I would rather summarize the whole event with the phrase "very intense." Maybe I should say that I liked what I felt, but I was uncertain about everything I saw. The event was very casual and very creative (people were doing different creative things all around the room), and the great variety of activity made me feel like anyone could come in. So I went in. The music was loud enough to cover most individual noise, but people were singing and speaking and playing instruments around the room. As I passed around the perimeter of the room I got mini concerts from each.

These people loved what they were doing.

These people were praying.

I felt very out of place.

I got the impression that everyone was having a personal conversation with someone, and the more I watched from the shadowy back corner the more I realized that they were having conversations with God. It was different. I wasn't sure what to do. I was not afraid to be there, but I wasn't sure how much longer I would stay. I could tell that it was a "religious" thing, but it just didn't feel like any church I had ever visited. It seemed very…real.

There was a band up front, but one guy didn't seem to be running the whole thing. People were not just repeating lines from some book. The whole group was involved in the singing and praying and dancing (no kidding), and the whole thing seemed to ebb and flow with a life of its own.

Behind the band, a huge mural was painted across the back wall of the stage. The color and line and concept were very familiar to me. I was sure I had seen the artist's work before. Across the huge, colorful mural were these words:

The Worship

The Worship Thoughts

Everyone worships. Every religion offers up a theory on what to worship. Every anti-religion offers up some worthy anti-idol as well.

Recently, while standing outside a temple in New Delhi, I asked a young woman what her religion taught her about worship. Her answer was an anti-choice theory that would allow all religions to share equal value on earth so that no one would ever have to choose just one. She said, "We think that God is our maker, so we always say prayers and meditate for that. We don't have any specific kind of worship. We only think that everyone can say their prayers according to how they feel. We say that here everyone can say their prayers according to their own beliefs."

What I learned on entering the temple was that she had omitted one very important worship rule: *all worshipers must be silent.* Only the sound of shuffling feet, creaking furniture, and the movement of the entrance and exit doors whispered around the room. Why silence? Because at the basis of this faith was the notion that all faiths are legitimate paths to God, and that no one way should be held higher than another. I know a lot of people who like this idea. Tragically, the end result of this belief system was that in public worship no one could express any conviction out loud because it would destroy the whole fantastic premise. The practical outcome of this premise was every belief being rendered mutually useless—they were not made equally advantageous. Worship was killed, and I am afraid so was God.

Followers of the Way have a unique worship practice. It is an embarrassingly open and honest worship. It is both public and private. It comes in many different forms and is practiced by different cultures all over the world. Though it is multicultural and multilingual, it does have a common focus. Followers of the Way worship the God who has rescued them in the person of Jesus Christ. There is no idol or icon that takes His place. There is no ritual or incantation that can steal the passion.

It is all about Jesus.

Their worship celebrates their initial encounter with Jesus, but they are not trapped in remembering the past. When they worship, they express an ongoing conversation with God—part of their ongoing connection. They laugh, cry, sing, and shout their hearts to God, and they listen for His reply. Their worship is focused not on religious devices but on pressing toward their ultimate goal of fully embracing and being embraced by God. In this "pressing" there is both spontaneous worship and planned worship. It is in this unguarded conversation that the complexity of the human condition is revealed. It is sometimes confused, sometimes certain, sometimes happy, sometimes angry, but in worship there is always honesty.

Their worship reflects intense thanksgiving for the way God has changed, and is changing, their lives.

Their worship is full of adoration for the God who has rescued them from the separation.

The Followers' worship is as creative and innovative as the God who inspires the romantic exchange.

And finally, all of this expression is poured out in full realization of the supernatural presence of God.

The Followers of the Way have discovered in Jesus Christ the way back to the joy of childhood—the discovery of eternal wonder— and they worship in response to every new thing they discover about Him.

Sacred Tattoo

The difference between this kind of vision and a dream is distinct. Dreams are whispers in comparison. For one, I was not asleep. In the vision I was fully aware, and I was fully able to comprehend the meanings and the actions of everything around me. Dreams change to accommodate the dreamer, but here, in the vision, I was the one who was changing.

When the Great Being stretched out His hands, I saw that my full name was written on the palm of His hand.

He smiled when I read it.

I wanted to smile as well, but the sweet sense of the moment was overshadowed by something I had not seen before. As he turned His arm to show where my name was written, the sleeve of His blood-red robe slipped down and revealed a gaping wound in His wrist. On the other wrist the same wound. A deep sadness surrounded me, everything faded to a purple and black mist, and I wanted to go away.

Why?

I knew what had caused the wounds.

In the distracting convulsions of the outer world, the bleak but busy world away from the great circle, no one ever noticed their inward self. I had paid no attention to mine. But here in the light, next to the peaceful beauty of the Great Being, I could not help but be ashamed. My heart was dark. It was guilt that had no alibi and remorse stronger than tears. I was not condemned from without but from within. My case was not a list of offenses or a specific trespass—I simply knew that *I was wrong*, and that my awful *wrongness* had cost Him these wounds.

I knew that many of those shouting and pointing and seething at the edge of the circle had felt the same dark sadness, but they refused the truth of it. They had turned the revelation on its head. In my ears I could hear their shouts of condemnation launched toward the center of the circle and all those who were in it. I knew they refused to accept the *wrongness*, and in their protest they were slipping out of their minds.

I could not protest. I realized as I stood at the edge of the beautiful circle that my name had always been written on His tender hand, but I had never once stopped to comprehend it. I knew that this Great Being had loved me from the time before I was. I knew that He had not removed my name even when I did not care that it was written. I knew that He had always thought lovingly of me even when I had thought nothing of Him at all. My wrong was not based on a broken law. My wrong was cut from a great love that was left unanswered—a devotion that was left hanging, forgotten, unreturned. Mine was the sin of indifference.

I still couldn't move my feet.

So I opened my mouth.

I spoke in a loud and quivering voice so all could hear, whether in or out of the circle. I confessed the reality of my life. I revealed my secret fears and desires. I opened up my guilt and shame of having never come to the Great Being before, and I acknowledged my sense of lack and helplessness. I pointed to my feet buried in the concrete, and while some jeered and some stood blank-faced, I confessed that I desperately wanted to come into the circle and join the rest but that I was powerless to do so. I shouted to what was behind me that I wanted no more part of the mindless activity of nothingness, and in my final passion I turned to the Great Being, who was still fully turned toward me and said…

Breath

I am the rush of warm air from the lips of the worshiping soul.

I fill the space between the consonants and roll underneath the vowels of the sacred transaction between man and God.

My presence separates thoughts from sounds. Under my power what once existed only as a thought in the secret place becomes a living thing that travels into the world—into the ears of men— into the ears of God.

I am the breath of worship.

I am more than words. I am the release of hidden things to God. The confession of lack and need and failure depend on me. I am how they find their mark. If these things are never given opportunity to partner with me then the inside of a person dries up and wastes away. As I escort the tragic cargo of broken things out of a person's inner home, the fresh, clean air from the heavens of God are drawn into the vacuum. They bring springtime to the barren landscape of the soul.

I am more than a transport for waste. I am also the friend of truth. I bring the beauty of truth, the eternal truths, into the world of the untrue across the lips of the worshiper. When I come spilling from the loving mouth I run quickly into the low places and find the foolishness of humanity and the wasting away of life…and I uncover them. I call for change. I draw the truth from the words on the pages of God's letter and give them transport into the earth.

The worshiper presses me underneath the words:

"All men are like grass, and all their glory is like the flowers of the field. The grass withers and the flowers fall, because the breath of the Lord blows on them. Surely the people are grass. The grass withers and the flowers fall, but the word of our God stands forever."

I fill the throat of the life in anguish. The broken heart that cries out to God needs me to express what is too deep for words. I do not depend on distinguishable shape or form. God knows not only what is made clear with words, but also what is behind the mysterious pressure and groan of each exhale.

To pour truth into the world and into the ears of God and the ears of men is a tireless work. As the worshiper inhales and prepares a worshipful thought, I begin my healing work. In the pause, in this moment of collection, I gather any broken things I might find in the worshiper's heart and tuck them away inside of my transport.

Exhale.

As the truth is carried along on my back, so is any unbelief— both of them dispelled from the body. The worshiper inhales and receives the fresh air from the world of God. I drop the false to roll away on the ground of the earth, and I carry the truth again into his ears.

We repeat all day. Driving. Walking. Resting.

Of all the work I am given to do, none is as sweet as to carry words of love into the very ears of God. I fold hot around the words of praise that are forced into the carpet underneath the prostrate worshiper's mouth. I escape around the face and hands of the worshiper and fly straight into the heavens. I cascade around heads of worshipers who release me into their private closets—places familiar with my travel.

Sometimes I am thrust with great force from a head thrown back in wild thanksgiving and echo off the walls of the buildings made by men, but I always escape to find the listening presence of God. In explosive bursts I leap from the mouths of dancing worshipers who are quick to inhale, and then quickly release me inside the rhythm of compliments and swirling, laughing praise.

I have poured from the mouths of both peasant children and wealthy kings. I fly to the same beautiful face and enter the same attentive ears.

Happy is the breath that finds purpose in bringing worship to God.

Woe is the breath trapped in the lungs of the dying proud.

Through The Mystical

God is touching us through the mystical.

Ghost stories and hauntings have long been part of our history. Fascination with unexplainable phenomena, whether on Easter Island or in our own community, is a common human theme. Prophets, fortune-tellers, and healers prove to us that reason alone may not encompass all of the human reality. The presence of the other world has been experienced as an evil force as well as a benevolent force. The question is not *if* there is a mystical reality, but *who* or *what* it is. The "who" and the "what" of the question should help us decide whether we should reach toward it or cautiously back away.

Western religion, almost without exception, has thrown out the supernatural in its quest to be rational. Too bad. Western religion has become irrelevant by doing so. Eastern religion has always embraced the supernatural, but today it is embraced *with a wink*, as if to say, "It's real, but don't take it too seriously." Many in the West are so desperate to try the Eastern versions that they fail to see the wink. Both views can kill our ability to hear God speaking through the transcendent things in life.

He is definitely mystical, and definitely reaching out to us.

To begin to sense His touch through the mystical, consider this Path of Seven. You may blend the experiments and improvise your own, but try to set apart at least fifteen minutes for each exercise. Try them individually over a span of time, and remember, you can come back to them even after you have finished the book.

1. Light a candle in the center of the room. Turn off all the lights. Sit near the candle by yourself, and close your eyes. You can see the flicker of the light through your eyelids, and your breathing is easy and deep. Open your mouth, and as you exhale say, "Living God, reveal Yourself to me." Repeat twenty times and then wait in silence for another ten minutes. It will feel like a long time.

2. Put a small notebook and pen near your side of the bed. Just before you fall asleep at night whisper, "Living God, will You speak to me tonight in my dreams?" At any point in the night, if you have an unusual dream grab the notebook and write it down. In the morning jot down any dream you can remember. After a week review the dreams and look for God in them.

3. Write down a brief account of the most important supernatural event of your life. It could be anything that has happened to you that was so unexplainable you have never forgotten it. Read the account out loud to God, and ask Him, "God, was that You?" Wait. If you sense it *was* Him, ask Him why He did it. Wait. Write down the answer.

4. Find someone who is a strong believer in God. Ask them to put a hand on your shoulder and pray something like this: "God, show Yourself to this person and prove how much You love them. Bring Your presence into their life right now, God, so that they can know You are here. Speak to their heart, God." Wait for a while. If you sense anything at all, tell the person about it.

5. Put on some music that puts you in a contemplative mood (no lyrics). Lie down on the floor and relax. Close your eyes. Say aloud, "God, tell me what You think of me." As soon as you see a picture of any kind (animal, figure, place, etc.) say, "I think You are telling me that I am like…" and ask God to

show you what He means through that picture.

6. Decide ahead of time that you are going to travel to a sacred place and meet with God. It can be any place you choose, but you have to warn God that you are going to meet Him there. Prepare yourself on the way to the sacred spot, and when you arrive you may only talk to Him for fifteen minutes and then pause to listen. No "talking to yourself." What is that like?

7. Have you ever seen a vision, or had a powerful picture enter your mind that seemed to be scripted and acted out for you? If you have ever been under the influence of drugs or alcohol (this is not a recommendation), did you ever hallucinate or have a vision that you still remember? Was it scary or peaceful? Write down the vision, and then write, "God, were You speaking to me through this vision?" Wait. Write down what you think the vision meant.

Ink

I am the flow of color pressed between the tip of the worshiper's pen and the paper that is dedicated to record every single movement.

I am driven from every impassioned thought. Each motion of the pen sends me streaming across the page in hopes of finding a word or phrase, or picture that will bring the worshiping heart to life.

There are sleeping places in the heart that cannot be awakened to speak—they are too shy to reveal themselves. There are uncertainties that can be uttered in an audible phrase, but my awesome power is to release these timid things through the conversation of writing.

At times I am poured so quickly from the tip of the pen that I can barely keep up with the expressions of joy and elation that the worshiper tries to express. I fly so swiftly across the paper that I can't get my footing on the texture of the page or catch my breath at the end of a thought. Instead of clear, determined lines I give way to the gestures of words and the intimations of feelings. Some words are reduced to tiny waves in the line, some whole phrases are lost in the rush, and often I run past the boundaries of the page left and right, above and below.

God reads the invisible intent as well as the actual script.

On other days the pressure of the pen is almost too much to bear. I suffocate under the weight of guilt, or anger, or repentance. On these pages my presence fills the deep grooves like black blood in the veins of regret. I have the courage to represent these things, however, because I am not afraid of punishment—I am certain of the kind of love that embraces both the sweet and the bitter of relationship.

As I leave my fluid impressions across the journal page of a person's worship I leave a trail of relationship and love. I enjoy the sentimental value of our history together. When I am closed away for the night I trace back through our relationship and enjoy the beautiful changes that have taken place in the life of the worshiper. Occasionally the writer might flip through the pages as well, finding memories that bring a steady assurance of the changing—things are becoming new.

Today, I am doing my best work. In the roughly handled book called the "Worship Journal" I am representing the poetry of the heart—love sonnets—the romantic language of affection. Written here are the words that cannot be spoken in public because they are reserved for the intimacies between lovers. It begins this evening in a locked room. The aromatic candles fill the air with a sacred sense of privacy. Under the single lamp on the old desk we flow:

The cross neither jewelry, nor icon, nor charm,

The cross held a lover who died in my arms...

Then furious page after page of loving words, the overwhelmed heart expresses its commitment. What had begun in the simple couplet had exploded into an unrestricted flow of words. Like thoughts delivered across ocean and battlefield to a distant lover I made the pages blush with every new paragraph I commissioned them to hold.

It is an amazing thing to write so perfectly what could never have been as well spoken.

It is also an amazing thing to hold those same thoughts so permanently on the page while the spoken words seem to drift hazily into the past. I hold the treasured thoughts so that both lovers can return and read them, anytime, anywhere.

Melting Prayers

Vision

What I said toward the Great Being from the edge of the circle I am still saying, but now I am moving. I feel light, and my feet are free to move again.

"Help me!" were the first words that fell from my mouth. The concrete around my feet had exploded into a spray of debris, and my whole body fell forward toward the brightness.

I am no longer buried in the *wrongness* outside the circle. As I speak I am also singing, and as I sing I am also shouting, and as I shout I am also weeping and laughing and falling all over the place...*inside the circle*.

The white-hot light shot through me and permeated everything in the vision. Time was entirely useless for the extended moment of my utterance and for what fell on me as I spoke. The remainder of my account is neither chronological nor haphazard—it is simply all of these things.

It is a strange thing to be divided and live. I was separated by the light that pierced me. I could clearly tell what was true and false. Just when I thought the realization would destroy me I saw that the light was coming from the mouth of the Great Being. From His mouth came words, a sharp blade, and light. All of them were running into me. At the point of the blade were my doubts, my opinions, and my façades, and they all melted—running down my legs and off of my feet into the ground.

Something stirred in me from a deep place. I had a faint memory of this place. It was like a personal myth that had been lost in childhood. I was transported to this inner retreat, and found myself in a lagoon hidden beneath waterfall and dense canopy. As I looked up from the waters of the pool and saw the sun for the first time, and as the warm light bathed me and the waters washed me, I was filled with such gratitude that I ran screaming and laughing onto the beach of this secret place. I kicked and skipped and yelled so that my voice echoed off the tall cliffs, "Thank You, thank You, Great Rescuing God, thank You!"

I had been rescued.

Yes!

I had been delivered! I had found peace! The peace had come from my confession, not from my denial, and it was such a release that I could not help but continue to thank Him over and over again.

His words, filled with light, began to rest in my heart. I found each one to be a treasure. I could hold each one and discover a thousand meanings—all of them true, and all of the truth ruled by His love. I knew it was love, because I was holding the word "love" in my hands. It was the word that flowed continually from the edge of the blade. All of the other words agreed with love, and no matter what order the words fell into my hands they always spoke of love.

As I held love in my hands, I saw others were holding it as well. We were holding it, kissing it, and speaking to it. There were poets standing on little boxes with love in one hand and their ragged writing books in the other, speaking beautiful phrases that rhymed all the words we had received. Painters working on huge canvases swept their brushes, filled with the colorful new words in intricate patterns, while singers all around blended their voices with what He had spoken. Potters, weavers, and builders were all creating works to honor and prove the strength of each word. All these sights and sounds and melodies harmonized with love.

On the inside I ran without growing weary around the secret place, and in my heart I found more and more reasons to thank the Great Being for His rescue, for His love, and for His words that were true.

On the outside, however, I could not arrange any complex language. I continued to speak in short, simple bursts of emotion toward the outstretched hand.

Arts

Meditation

I am perfectly still.

I am active, but unmoving. My motion is not found in physical activity but in the exchange of life between the heavens and the body of the worshiping soul.

I am the quiet intent—the repetition of the worshiping heart.

I am meditation.

My focal point is in the heavens, not behind the doors of tiny altars, or inside the great doors of cathedrals. I do not find my love in the pages of a sacred book or in sacred teachings or sacraments. My embrace is not satisfied with a cold icon or religious symbol.

My affection is not for the crucifix made of wood, but the God who came to show His love for humanity on it. He is the One who rose from the dead. It is He who meets me in the silence and it is He who calls to me in the storm.

I am ancient.

In the ancient kingdoms they said, "Within your temple, O God, we meditate on your unfailing love." The prophet commanded my posture: "Be still before the Lord, all mankind, because he has roused himself from his holy dwelling."

Surrounding the head of the worshiping soul I give rest to the mind. The mind is a busy train station, a room full of children. In me there is stillness. The stillness begins when the worshiper shuts away all the business of the day outside the room of meditation or to the edge of the quiet field. This is often inspired with some whispering release: "I will meditate on all Your works and consider all Your mighty deeds."

When the truth encircles the mind, then the body can rest.

The body always gives voice to the inner man. If the inner man is frightened the body shrinks. If the inner man is worrisome then the body wrings its hands. But when the inner man trusts God then the body is brought under the discipline of stillness.

When the heart sits down then so can the body.

If the eyes are not anxiously looking about for things that have been lost, then the heart can close its eyes and be still as well. When the heart listens for God, then the body can ignore the tyranny of urgent sounds. I am expressed in a myriad of physical ways: sitting, prostrate, in the Lotus, and with folded hands. I lie back in the grass, and I stand still on the mountain.

I find myself recommended by the music of peaceful artists, the soothing smells of incense or aromatics, and the rustling of the wind in the open fields and mountains and streams of the earth. I encircle those who have learned to practice my posture, and I release them from anxiety into the healing presence of Christ.

Just like the act of holding hands can make way for the understanding of friendship, the act of expressing stillness can make way to intimacy with God.

I roll like a blanket of rest around the shoulder of the seated worshiper. I lay my hands on the head of the prostrate seeker. I kiss the fingers of the kneeling one in the prayers of waiting: "Be still before the Lord," I whisper, "and wait patiently for Him," and then I transport the trusting soul into the quieting presence of Jesus.

The walls of this universe still vibrate with the words of the master to the roaring waves, "Quiet! Be still!" and the waters of the heart still obey…even the distant echo of the command.

I show the worshiper how his hands are held tightly in the hands of the master. I show him the fields of enjoyment around the presence of God, and I loose his imagination to discover the beauty of Christ. It is my greatest joy to see the joy on the worshiping face that stays long enough to find the quiet power of God.

Seconds become minutes, minutes become hours, and hours become a way of life for the pursuing heart. The wonders of God transcend all understanding, and they warm the heart and mind.

I am the pleasing meditation on the wonders of God.

The Quiet Cup

"Worship is a conversation with God."

I repeated the phrase from the business card in my mind as I scanned the crowd of people. I half expected a small room with a guy in the front talking *about* worship. It was not like that at all.

They were really going at it.

I was still unfamiliar with the whole idea of actually *worshiping,* and during this first introduction I never really stopped to make any judgments. I just took it all in.

A lot of kinetic activity was going on around the front and middle of the room, but where I stood there was a pocket of more reserved people. Several were sprawled out on the floor with drawing paper, and they swept the colored pencils and chalk all over the surface. Some were sitting with their legs crossed, pen in hand, with ragged journals laid out on their laps. I could see that some of these "writers" sat with their eyes closed as though they were listening for someone, while others bent over their papers writing and reading their own lines. This was definitely not the first time for some of them because they had several books in different colors and bindings laid all around them. They would grab one and write, put it down, then grab another, like they were placing different thoughts from the "muse" on the different pages of their journals.

To my left, just in front of me, a girl was laid out flat on the floor. It looked as if she had crashed through some chairs to end up where she was, but at the moment she looked very peaceful. She had a faint smile on her face. Her eyes were closed, and her hands rested on her skirt lying loosely around her. Maybe she was just listening to the music?

Across the room several people stood in front of large canvases, using large brush strokes and lots of color. One guy was using his hands, and the easel rocked back and forth as he pressed into his work. This was not an orchestrated thing; it seemed more like some sort of visual improvisation—like a good jazz concert where each artist releases the inspiration at the right time. I decided it was spontaneous because of the abstract nature of some of the work, and the fact that the painters' movements seemed to cooperate with the rise and fall of the rhythm and music. Along with the painters' movements were the movements of people dancing, and clapping, and singing.

It seemed less like a performance than it did a conversation.

Then the music changed. The volume came way down and I could hear someone reading. No, actually everyone was reading. It started kind of low and then grew in strength. I think it may have been a passage from the Bible, but I didn't see everyone flipping through them. Glancing toward the front I saw that the words were projected on screens so we could all read them. I began to mouth along,

> "...the Lord, who remains faithful forever. He upholds the cause of the oppressed and gives food to the hungry. The Lord sets prisoners free, the Lord gives sight to the blind, the Lord lifts up those who are bowed down, the Lord loves the righteous. The Lord watches over the alien and sustains the fatherless and the widow...."

And with that the music stopped.

Silence.

No one moved, unless they were bending over or kneeling on the floor. I could barely hear some of the people near me repeating lines from what we had just read. Some said absolutely nothing. And in a few moments no one was speaking at all, no one was even whispering, and the room was unearthly still.

In the hush I began to feel something very new to me. It was as if a weight had been placed over the whole room, and I was able to feel it along with everyone else. It was a very serious feeling that made me want to do something, but I couldn't decide what to do. I could kneel down, but that didn't make sense to me then. I could just stand there and pretend nothing was happening, or maybe I could squeeze out the back door and get some relief from the strange sensation.

I opted for the back door escape plan.

As I turned slowly to go I had to step over a person or two to make it back to the door. One of the their writing notebooks lay open, and I couldn't help but read the large black title:

Killing The Old God

To choose to worship God is not an entry into a coded textbook of religious activity, nor an affiliation with a system of behaving. It is a mystical step into His presence with both eyes open. If knowing God begins with a real encounter, we should feel free to throw off the old stereotypes we have forced Him to wear. Reaching out to God is a natural and necessary step in the life of someone who feels God reaching out to them. If we can sense His hand extended to us through the world around, then the question is, will we leave it empty, or will we reach out to touch it in return?

One of the most destructive mistakes in the growth of any relationship is to allow assumptions about a person's character to affect the personal discovery process. Sometimes it is a bad first impression that molds a false judgment. Sometimes it is stereotyping that kills the relationship before it can begin. The answer is, of course, to get to know someone personally.

In some cases a pile of misinformation, stereotypes, and bad first impressions has to be worked through before a serious relationship can develop.

"I thought everyone who did that was..."

"He acted like that other guy and so..."

"Before we met I heard that she..."

One of the most popular God-stereotypes for religious people is the "Cosmic Policeman." This is the God who has a whistle in one hand and a large stick in the other. He not only blows the whistle when we do something wrong, he dishes out our punishment with a whack from the happy stick of pain. To make things worse, the whistle, the pointing finger, and the whack are done in broad daylight so that everyone can see. The Cosmic Policeman gets his jollies by humiliating us in public. Occasionally, through the groveling and crying of the "busted," he might show mercy, but it is probably just to induce a much-needed favor. He might even say, "There's going to be hell to pay if I catch you doing that again. I made you. I can make another one just like you!"

He can't really be like this can He? If this were His true nature, what would it say about the meaning of life, the value of creation, the future of our world? How do you see God?

Pope-Meets-Santa Claus?

Distant cloud of nothingness?

Carl Sagan's nemesis?

Omnipotent retiree?

Have you ever wondered where these stereotypes come from? First impressions? Secondhand information? Fairy tales? If we want to move closer to Him, we will have to kill these stereotypes and get to know the *real* Him, not the imagined Him. We will have to demand that He be all that God must really be.

Supernatural.

Endlessly wonderful.

The Lovely.

The Perfect.

The Perfect Lover.

Could He be God and be anything else? Then why settle for less?

Many of us have layers of stereotypes that we force God to wear. Wouldn't it be great if He could come to the party dressed as He really is? We might discover something beautiful behind the hearsay.

Forgiving God

God has broken many hearts. God has failed many expectations. God has ruined many people's lives. God has ordered the death of many innocents. God has forgotten the homeless. God has unleashed evil on the earth. God is corrupt.

So the story goes.

Do you buy it?

If you do, we are all in a terrible mess. Life has a corrupt beginning, a flawed present, and a hopeless end. This would *not* be a tragedy we could write about like some dark poet removed from the reality of the drama. There would be no chance to rise above it and gather a rhyming thought; we would be submerged in it.

If you do not buy it, there must be something wrong with our perception. Maybe our perception is *limited*? Just because we cannot understand every move of the Maker we are not entitled to remove Him from the reality of life—even if the reality of life seems flawed and full of inconsistencies and full of evil.

Many philosophers have tried to prove the non-existence of God by using the existence of evil as their proof-text. Without exception they all *have to pretend* to be removed from humanity like an innocent bystander to state their theory of denial. Why? Because the question of evil *in the world* points to the question of evil *in the one making the judgment*. So, if evil exists it has certainly affected our own ability to properly judge God.

Maybe our perception is twisted like an image through warped glass. Small tragedies, little disappointments, and unanswered questions pile one upon the other on the surface of the glass until nothing makes sense anymore. God is out there somewhere, or maybe just on the other side, but we can't make out a clear outline anymore. It is just too hard to understand Him, so forget it.

God needs our forgiveness.

These same kinds of offenses—sometimes intentional, sometimes accidental—often separate lifelong lovers. The romance has a good ending only if they learn these priceless truths along the way:

Sometimes forgiveness is better than understanding.

Sometimes forgiveness is superior to reason.

Sometimes forgiveness is the key to healing the eyes.

God needs to be forgiven.

How has God offended you? How has He let you down? How is God not doing what He should be doing? Or should have done? Tell Him. Do you think He can handle it? Maybe He needs to let us pound His chest and slap His face until things begin to make sense again, or at least until we have exhausted our anger. Most people discover that when they move close enough to see His face, even in the rage of misunderstanding, that there is something to learn. They discover the unexpected God. Stereotypes began to melt from the heat of His compassion and the washing of His tears. How He reacts to human pain makes a difference.

If we don't forgive Him for what He has done or what He has

not done, we will always be trapped in our bitterness and we may never know Him. We must find a way to forgive if we are going to know Him better. Maybe as we move in closer and choose to speak the truth, whether pleasant or harsh, we will find that honesty is the key to any good relationship, even a relationship with God.

Finding The Beautiful

More than one relationship has been saved from impending doom (or at least terrible mediocrity) by the wonderful gift of the unexpected compliment. However silly that may sound, the *unexpected compliment* goes a long, long way. Praise is a healer of wounds. A gesture of adoration in a moment when it is not looked for can make a person's day. Doesn't everyone love a rich compliment? We are not talking about the patronizing stuff designed to manipulate a situation—we are talking about real adoration.

One sure way to build a bridge into the presence of God is to practice the art of the spontaneous compliment. Even the most difficult person has at least one admirable quality to compliment. God has an infinite number of wonderful things to adore. Finding them can become a lifelong sport.

The simplest way to build the bridge to God through compliments is to recognize the things He has done well. It is the same in any relationship. When we first get to know someone we can't speak our appreciation for the deep things in their life, so we begin by commenting on the things they obviously do well:

"You are a good listener. I really appreciate it."

"You are really in shape. Do you work out?"

"It's been a long time since I met a person who is so organized!"

Little things count. People who want to touch a real God might need to start with a patient understanding of the relationship's progress. Start small. Go carefully. Ask questions. Expect answers. Compliment. Offer thanks for little things. The person who looks for the positive things in the life of a new friend will usually find them.

Admiring someone can open the door to a new part of his or her life. Often they let their guard down in the face of appreciation and praise.

They let us in a little further.

What follows is a Path of Seven for rediscovering God. These exercises can help clear the path of old stereotypes into the true nature of God. In these we can remove the bitterness of unforgiveness. They can also help wash the face of God so we can see Him better. Don't be in a hurry to complete them all at once.

1. In a quiet place write down this question: Why would an artist count any brush stroke as a waste of time? Underneath it write: How could the God who created everything not care deeply for everything He created? Write a short answer for each. Does the answer say anything about how He must feel about you?

2. Find a high place. As you look out over the horizon consider the vastness of God. Pick up a rock and hold it in one hand. Consider the way God has often been small enough to fit in your pocket when you needed Him. Ask God why He doesn't react harshly when we treat Him like an optional thing.

3. Take out a piece of paper. Describe how God has offended you, or let you down, or failed to come through. Find a quiet

place and ask God to show you where He was and what He was doing during the offenses. Write down what you sense Him saying.

4. Draw a picture of God. What does He look like? Does He wear a robe? Why? Is He threatening? Why? What is around Him? Why? Has God communicated any of these characteristics to you through a trustworthy agent? If not, where did you learn them?

5. Walk in a garden and ask yourself aloud: How could God possibly love only religious people? Does God love everyone or only some? Why? If He loves us all the same, then what happens to His heart if some love Him in return and others do not?

6. While driving alone in your car, say out loud, "God, I refuse to believe the slander about You without testing it for myself. I also refuse to believe that You do not exist because I have been raised a skeptic. God, I want You to reveal Yourself to me personally, and until You do so I realize that I have no right to pre-judge You with partial history or secondhand theory."

7. Walk through a mall. People make a lot of stuff, don't they? Think of the things God has made that really impress you. Spend some time telling God how great you think some of His creations are. Try to go on and on about the miracle of their existence and beauty.

Arts

Song

I tickle the mouths of babies and school children.

I roll from the mouths of men and women on every continent of the earth.

I fill the world with sound. I ride on the melody released from the body of the worshiping soul. My words are filled with loving intent.

I am the worshiping song.

I have intertwined the melody and rhythms of a thousand peoples. I have made a home in the lives of people of every tone of skin: browns, amber, olives, and cream. I love the fusion of true love and the resonance of wood, string, and reed. I love the fusion of cultures and rhythms from the corners of the earth come to worship Christ. The choirs of nations will unfold me.

When I am young I am read from books, sometimes sheets of paper or projection screens. My work has survived on the lips of the living through beautiful repetition.

I am also conceived and born on the minute and second of every tick of the clock. Sometimes born an infant. Sometimes born full-grown. My age is not based on the sophistication of language, or the complexity of the melody. My maturity is not dependent on the passing of years. My full maturity is realized when the vocalist reaches deep into the soul and draws out pure, honest conversation with God.

The Muse of my inspiration does not exist in mythology, but in the object of my affection. The Spirit of the God I adore is the same Spirit that draws me from the worshiper's heart. The Writings say, "Do you not know that your body is a temple of the Holy Spirit, who is in you, whom you have received from God?" The worshiping heart does not go to a building to find God, nor does it go to a book to find me, but reaching inside it discovers that both the object of its affection and the ability to express love through me is always present!

I can feel this amazing Spirit forming me, calling to me, sending me out. I hear heavenly melodies, sometimes simple, sometimes intricate, and I explode into the imagination of the worshiper in picture, in word, and in rhythm. This loving Spirit sends me out a million times a day. The worshiper can endlessly say, "He put a new song in my mouth, a hymn of praise to our God."

I create melody and rhythm when released into space. I dance out into the room and call others to join me in harmony and countermelody. I make the chest compress and the whole body vibrate with my expression, and I reveal the deep things of the heart to God and the deep things of God to the worshiper.

Today, I ache with desire.

To be poured out into the ears of God.

A deep, honest exchange with God wrapped in melody:

I am the worshiping song.

Thoughts
Worship Is Conversation

If there is one thing all of us need, it is the ability to have conversation with God.

There have been times when I have felt like a prisoner in isolation, locked away in a pit with no chance of hearing or being heard. Many times I have felt like a castaway striking signal fires in hopes that He may see me from the distance. I spell my name in the sand in case He remembers it, and my soul writes an SOS on the beach. I used to believe that He sat on the other side of a confessional screen listening to me blather on, but He could only speak to me in truisms and bumper stickers.

If God would only speak.

In the middle of my cry, in the middle of my search, in the middle of my dissatisfaction *I found Him*. In His hands He held a note first written by His prophet thousands of years ago: "Can a mother forget the baby at her breast and have no compassion on the child she has borne? Though she may forget, I will not forget you! See, I have engraved you on the palms of my hands…"

I was destroyed!

What could this mean? Could God have been sending up signal fires for me? Was the cross of Christ the fuel for the flame? Had the nails in His hands and feet created the tattoos of pain by which He remembered me?

In retrospect, I think that it was *He that found me*.

Just how did I end up in the pit of isolation? How did I come to be lost in the sea of separation from Him? And then the prophet spoke again, "Surely the arm of the Lord is not too short to save, nor His ear too dull to hear. But your iniquities have separated you from your God; your sins have hidden His face from you, so that He will not hear. For your hands are stained with blood, your fingers with guilt...."

Before we can connect to the presence of God we have to find a way to be honest with ourselves about the tragic state of our hearts.

We have forgotten God.

We have pursued life in every corner of the earth, but we have not pursued life with Him. The Creator stands amazed, and He hangs brokenhearted, wishing and waiting for our return. At least He did not stand silent! In fact God has proven Himself to be the tireless communicator. Of course, it has been very difficult to hear Him with all the things we have stuffed in our ears, but, nonetheless, He has been working to speak to us. Jesus said so clearly in the picture of a gentle shepherd, "My sheep listen to my voice; I know them, and they follow me." If He is still speaking, have we been listening?

He has called to us in nature, in dreams, in the beauty of the world. He has shouted through the pain and frustrations of life. He has written an intense letter of love to us that is filled with promises of commitment and rescue, and in all these things we are just learning to hear Him. But we must press on! A fantastic treasure awaits those who come to know that they can hear His voice and feel His touch—it is the ability to have conversation with God!

So much breath passes from our bodies every day, and much of it fails to carry any words of worth into the world. I am choosing now to save some for Him. I am looking for words of thanks to exhale. I am looking for phrases to repeat that will fill the world around me with the whispered truth of God's presence. I am intent to inhale His words to me. Some of these words I read from pages of the Bible, and I repeat them until they fill the mouth of God in my mind. Some of them I hear Him speak in visions as I walk and talk with Him, and some of His words I hear at night in my dreams. I hold them in my heart and repeat them back to Him. I am reflecting my Lover's words in the mirror of my worship to make sure, by the look on His face, that they are really true.

Because I am a novice I often find it difficult to know how to speak, so I write. I take my thoughts of love and questions of relationship and put them down in my journal and into the margins of my Bible. What fills the margins of my prayer journals will soon become the text of my open conversation with God, but for now it is enough simply to pen the exchange. I write down the things I feel. I write down the things I need. I spend a great deal of time complimenting and appreciating what I discover of Him.

What I love about this conversation is that it is slow and deliberate. I have grown so tired of brief, meaningless conversations with the bank teller, the mailman, and the waiter. I enjoy the patient way that God and I relay our thoughts to one another on the printed page. I also love being able to review our previous conversations and break new ground with Him as we grow to know one another better.

I assume the posture of silence to hear the voice of God. I have been confused by the many voices that try to invade my world from the city street and the conversations of strangers. I want the windows of my mind to be shut to the traffic of confusion and focused on the God who has come to live in me! In the private place, I will listen for the inner voice of God. He promised to come and live in me, so why should I go looking for Him in buildings? Why should I look to a symbol or another person? I have embraced Christ, I have confessed my own failure, and I have asked God to come and live in me. He has been true to His promise!

Worship is conversation. Conversation is a two-way exchange of thought with the intent to discover. God speaks to us to discover every part of us. We speak to Him to discover Him in all His wonder and all His love for us.

Breathe Him.

Write Him.

Meditate Him.

Music

I am constantly trespassing the boundaries that confine the language of words.

I am passion given voice.

I am the music of the worshiping soul.

I explode from the impact of sticks upon drumheads and tonal carvings. I resonate from the bodies of instruments drawn taut with strings. I pierce the defenseless air from the stress of vibrating horns made of brass and wood. I exist because of physical conflict. I exist to bring the physical world out of conflict and into the order of God.

I am the rhythm of worship.

I use the frustrated reed, the stress of turned metal, and the conflict of the striking hammer to bring beauty—not disfigurement—into the audible world. I can bring deliverance to the wounded soul.

As the heart beats and signifies life, but does not contain life, I also signify the moving passion of worshiping people, but I do not fully contain the passion. My deep work is to reflect the feelings in the heart, to release the emotion of the gathering, and to give physical expression to the spiritual world.

I am conflict submitted to God, and I sound beautiful.

I am tension released to relationship with Christ, and I feel wonderful.

I exist in the heavens, in the spiritual world that some men never see, and I move like a great tide from the throne room of God into the rooms of worshipers everywhere. My distant half-brothers fill the earth with reflections of love for *everything but* the living God. They are only half-rhythms and half-music, and they only hint at the sacred, even if pointing to the profane. I am pure. Whether aggressive or sublime. Whether future or primeval. Whether simple or confused. I can be angry or sad or lonely or happy or insane or romantic. I am the sound of relationship between people and God.

I celebrate the joy of marriage. I draw tears from the eyes of babies. I call dancing from the feet of elders. I echo through the forests of every continent. I live carefully in private rooms. When the Spirit of God moves in me, then the simplest of beats, the most monochromatic tone, can invoke visions and reveal mysteries to men. God speaks through me. I am a mouthpiece with no mouth. I am a two-way street emotional exchange between God and the worshiping soul.

As I fall from the rhythm of one worshiper's drum I run across the circle to another drummer's hands. I call up shakers and bells to agree with me, and I can be answered or countered or duplicated by any worshiper who understands the way I feel. I move through the guitar and the flute and the violin and give storytelling melody to the communal event. Some hear my message, and some hear only the instrument.

I tell of God's aggressive love.

I throw myself at the Pursuing Lover.

I speak frankly of the passion that aches to be released from the worshiper's heart.

I open the door to the permanent world of eternity. I am the music of worship.

Pleasures Of God

"Forgive me!" were my next audible words.

Aware that this wonderful love had cost me more than I could ever pay, I cried for mercy. There would be no appeal to a higher court. I wrote a full confession and threw the documents toward the center for all to see my broken life.

My confessions scattered in the wind of the worshiping peoples and creatures. Afraid to land on the ground, they drifted around the heads of the old men who cried "Holy, Holy, Holy" and the creatures who were singing the song "Worthy is the Lamb who was slain." They fell in plain view of all.

Then the Great Being moved.

Swiftly.

Gathering all the documents in one wide, flowing gesture He folded them away under His blood red robe. They were instantly gone from view. I could tell He took pleasure at having covered the confessions.

He was glad to have hidden my shame.

When His hand came out from behind the robe He was holding, not the confessions, but a new, white robe.

I was completely naked. My confessions had unraveled all the old garments I had wrapped myself in and they were burning away into nothing. In the same way my confessions had cascaded around the throne, the smoke from my old stained clothes was whirling around the worshipers and filling the place like some rare incense. The smell was not what I would have expected; it was sweet like a rose.

He laid the new white robe around my shoulders.

The white of the robe was like the white of the horse stamping underneath the Great Being. It was like the white of the garments of the creatures and the old men and the other worshipers. It was like the white of the Great Being's hair, the clothes of the armies, the white of the great throne, and the stone I held in my hand.

The stone had my new name written on it.

Everything was new, and I fell down on my knees, then on my face, and I loved the Great, Merciful, Forgiving Being. As I pressed myself low before Him I returned every emotion of thanks and amazement to Him. As I thought more deeply about my forgiveness and the white of my robe, I pressed harder into the low place of my heart and found great joy in being lower and lower and lower.

The lower I went the more wonderful He became, and soon I realized what I had not fully realized before. In all the rescue, in all the forgiveness, and in all the worship I had not fully understood who He really was.

Seven
Choosing

It doesn't take long to grow weary when traveling down the road of self-improvement. Whether the do-it-yourself kit is newly packaged in a "formula for financial success" wrapper or in the popular "cult of ancient wisdom" tape series the results are the same: tiredness. If these kind of formulas worked, of course, our messed up world would have been put back in order long ago, and the unrest in our hearts would have long since been put to bed. It's odd that given their proven inadequacy we still remain oddly attracted to "work hard and do it yourself" religious activities. It must have something to do with our inability to admit that we are sick, and the deadly illusion that we have the power to fix everything.

After choosing *humility*, another adjustment we have to make in our posture when we choose to believe in God is our decision to be *helpless*. We need to admit and believe that we desperately need help.

The desire to find meaning and order in life is honorable. The desire to be in harmony with creation is admirable. The will to control the unruly passions of the body is necessary. But what will be our means to accomplish the end? Can we do it ourselves? The brokenness in the world points to our need for help. The dysfunction *inside* of us is paralleled by the chaos *outside* of us as well. How can we, through self-effort, fix what we did not create in ourselves or in the world around us? We did break it, but do we know how to put it back together properly?

People love to fix things, and many have submitted plans for us to fix our world. Wise men have espoused meditation on a better world. Sages have brought systems of order and discipline. Prophets have spoken regulation and ritual to the nations. Teachers have designed methods to understand the corners of human existence. And many other religions have exampled brave attempts to fix what is wrong inside of our own hearts.

But what if we were created?

What if we have no key within ourselves to unlock the door for healing? What if the broken can't fix themselves...because they are truly broken?

If we choose to believe in God, then shouldn't we believe that He could help us? If He loves us, and He made us with good intentions, wouldn't it only make sense that He has a plan for our rescue, for our healing?

The best kind of God, a caring God, would not just send a messenger or a book to rescue us from our chaos—He would attend to our deep wounds personally.

Go watch the lives of people who are into the "do-it-yourself" religions. They are constantly looking for private escapes for pleasure—little interludes of personal vacation from the treadmill of religion. All of our self-help religion will leave us breathless.

I, personally, have decided I need help, and I am going to worship the God who will help me out of the hole I am in, offer a real answer for how the hole got there to begin with, and provide a sure way to avoid falling back in!

When we approach God we choose to be *humble*, which is agreeing with our real position in the universe, and then we choose to be *helpless*, which is agreeing with our true power (or lack thereof) in the created world. Next comes the question of our need to be *honest*.

I know I have broken the rules.

What rules? Self-imposed religious rules?

No.

I am talking about the internal sense we all have that some things are good and some things are definitely not good.

I tread in the territory of the *definitely not good* a lot of the time. I do what I do not want to. I don't do what I know I should. I think about the forbidden. I fail to consider the needful. I don't need a religious book to tell me that I am not quite right.

Anyone who is going to approach God should get serious about honesty—telling the truth about "me." The truth is often not very pretty. Sure, we have been many times broken...but we also do a lot of breaking. The fact is that we have so screwed up our own lives, and cumulatively screwed up society, that it is amazing we have the ability to survive the consequences. We are fast running out of things to blame for our own broken state. We hire broken lawyers to defend our broken actions and point broken fingers to blame broken parents, and we watch television glorifying broken people cheating on broken people who watch the broken earth swallow up thousands of broken victims on the latest broken reality show.

Could we just be honest?

I, personally, am ready to make confession.

I am broken.

God must already know this, so maybe our need for confession is more for us than it is for Him. Confession is more than a spiritual tradition—it is the beginning of a relationship. Maybe it is necessary so that we can shake hands with God without any masks of pretense. Being ourselves—even our broken-selves—is the only way to have an honest relationship with God.

I have decided that in both public and private settings I must be honest with God. I must confess my needs and my failures and my sense of wrongdoing and wrong-being. It is my hope that by clinging to reality instead of a weak defense, God will prove His love for me by coming to my rescue.

God, I choose to be honest, helpless, and humble.

The following is a Path of Seven that may help us move closer to God. This is a *posture evaluation*.

1. Make a list of all the religious things you do, the rituals to find God's favor. While holding the list ask God out loud, "Do these things really make You love me more? What if I don't do them—will You love me less?"

2. Stand in a wide, open place. Apart from most modern conveniences, try to count on both hands the number of things you depend on at that moment for life. Try to tell yourself that you are "all powerful." Laugh out loud as long as you can.

3. Look toward the sky as if God were there. (The sky seems good because it is big.) Tell Him about how big He must be and how small you feel. If you can, tell God about the things in your life that make you feel helpless.

4. Make a list of all the things in your life that make you feel guilty. The things that you know are not right. The things you can't stop, but you want to. Hide the list. Ask yourself if the things will go away if you just ignore them. Ask yourself if the *wrongness* in your life seems to be weak and temporary,

or strong and permanent.

5. Search for Alcoholics Anonymous on the Web. Read the Twelve Steps. Do they make sense to you? Do you ever wish you could have your own private Twelve-Step Group without having to go "public" with what you hate about yourself?

6. Say aloud, "God, if You are real, please be a loving God! Please be a forgiving God! Please be a personal, rescuing God!" How does that feel? This could be a great time to tell God that You really need His help.

7. Think of some arrogant people who make you sick. Think of how they must be terribly confused about reality to be so proud. Write out on paper, "I forgive _____ for being so confused about reality and being so arrogant. God, help them to see clearly. Help me to be humble." Repeat until all the names you can think of have been put in the blank.

Visual

I am ground into powder, pressed into nothing, mixed with the world, and through conversation I become a living thing.

I am the color and form and texture of the crafted vision.

I am the visual art of worship.

Under the crushing force of the pestle and mortar my colors are made fine and pure: amber, indigo, and crimson. Hidden away in tubes, bags, and cans I am drawn from my holding cells and released into the light for all to see. Placed in waiting on the palette, however, the pain of my creation fades in my memory as I await the fulfillment of my dream—to find my place in expression to God. It is a delight to fall under the hands of children at play, and even greater to be unleashed from the hands of skilled worshiper. Discipline of craft and purpose bring alive the potential I possess for a conversation of love.

Pulled from the earth's grip I am sifted and reduced, moistened and renewed, and then smashed down on the center of the spinning wheel or pressed onto the hard, smooth platform. The fingers of the worshiping artist will leave their memory in me. All the people of the earth enjoy my submission to their imagination, old and young alike, but to feel the determined hands of the worshiping artist is to be given more than a dream—it is to be given a worthy life!

I teach the artist the character of God.

I teach rhythm, balance, perspective, and light—each of them a guidepost to His nature. In the process of being revealed I teach patience, order, timing, and rest. As we grow together I ultimately provide a doorway for the artist to reach into the world and find beauty—to find the story of God. My story is introduced to the world on the canvas, the pedestal, the wall, or the suspension. I am more than a mirror to the chaos of the world around us; I am a window into the healing intentions of the saving God.

Carefully I grow. Not too fast. In the gathering of believers I love to find a place to speak of the glory of God. Come and watch me from beginning to end. I love to remove the white canvas from its lonely position. Come and see if you can read my mind before I harden in a final, frozen thought. In the public square I love to emerge from the lifeless mass to a living form—a metamorphosis on display. Come and discover the insights I reveal as I emerge— insights I might not even reveal to the hands that form me.

Exposing myself to all, whether welcomed or misunderstood, I am a defenseless work. Say of me what you will. I will say of you what I must. When I become transparent and naked to reveal the majesty of God, blushing humanity will not reveal my shame, but their own. As I cast new light on the beauty of God I will also cast light on the pathway for the seeker to come and find Him.

Let me out, worshiping artist!

Set me free from the confines of tradition!

The fear of man is not in me! I must speak boldly of the beauty of God and call all peoples to consider their ways, for my purpose is not to be looked upon, but to do the looking. I will search the heart of man with my own eyes, and when the true or the false is discovered I will hold it up as a mirror to the earth.

The only eyes that can judge me are the eyes of the Creator— the Master Craftsman, the Divine Artist.

For His pleasure I live.

For His smile I mature.

So I set my worshiping master to the task. I am a wonderful obsession. I call him to shape my mouth to speak love words to God. I demand that he bend my body in humble gesture before Christ. Contrary to tradition I am not the artist's commission, but he is mine—and I will train him to worship God!

House Blend

Falling through the doors toward the coffee stand made me feel much better.

Something familiar would be good.

I had been in the room long enough to know that no one was going to point me out or make me do anything strange. I knew I could be a perfectly comfortable observer, but I was not perfectly comfortable with that heavy feeling that was pressing into me. As I dropped one sugar cube in my coffee I thought two things. "Wow, these people use cubes," and, "I wonder if that heavy feeling has to do with worship...or with God?"

No sooner had that thought left my brain than a hand touched my elbow and a polite voice said, "Hi, I'm Chris."

The conversation that followed was amazing. This was the "Chris" of the psycho coffeehouse art, and she met my expectations.

Polite, but very straightforward. Quirky, but very attractive.

She was easy to talk to. Our interaction moved effortlessly from coffee to the civic theater to her interest in climbing and my recent grad school experience, and before I could stop the progress of my mouth I told her about my struggle toward some kind of spiritual understanding. I couldn't believe it. Right there in front of the "House Blend" I used the words "God" and "espresso" and "struggle" in the same conversation.

I had just met this girl.

Her response was unique. Rather than chase down my thoughts and speak to each of them (or just run away...which I half expected), she simply said, "Well, I have learned that talking about God doesn't answer the heart as fast as actually talking to Him. That's why we do this..." She paused for a moment as she gathered some of her things.

"I hope you will come back?" she said just before she waved and disappeared through the doors back into the room of worshipers.

I decided that she was not flirtatious or artificial. I did want to go back, and I did want to see her again.

I don't know exactly why I stayed, but I decided I would go back in and find a seat with a view—and, at least, be a safe voyeur.

When I entered the room everyone was clapping. One person had just stepped down from the microphone and another was just stepping up. He opened his ragged writing notebook and with no introduction began to read. What fell from his mouth was some poetry, some prose, and it was filled with anger and question and relief. I was amazed by the fact that, in this obviously spiritual gathering, people were allowed to take the microphone and talk so frankly about what they didn't understand or what they genuinely hated. This guy was dealing with something, but his poem was about asking for help, and everyone in the room seemed to understand.

As people applauded I looked around the room. The lighting changed to focus on a little stage to one side that I had not seen before. A girl, sitting at a potter's wheel, was talking about feeling God's hands on her life. She spoke with the same ease that her hands moved the clay at her fingertips. Hypnotic. She was saying things about God's creativity and her need to be shaped, challenged, and broken. Then everyone began to sing a song following the lyrics on the screen.

The stage quickly filled with people holding hand drums and weird instruments. They were mostly sitting on the floor and around the edges of the stage. The song grew from what was written and became more like a chant. I even joined in as we sang the song that had filled the room with its simple phrase:

HIS LOVING ARMS
AROUND US,

HIS LOVING WORD
SURROUNDS US.

Worship Is Celebration

Wild and loose.

Love can be wild and loose.

Sound scary? Sound fun? I like the way it reminds me of my new relationship with God. It reminds me of worship—the way I can express the energy of my love to God.

Some shrink back at the thought of expressing emotion to the God of the Bible, but that is because they have never met the God of the Bible. They have trusted the barren relationship of others to feed their souls with dusty tradition. They have learned to call an empty house a home. Those who have been forgiven, those who have touched His face, cannot help but burst into loving song and dancing rhythm!

He did not buy us a house that we could occupy with our rule-books and rituals. Christ made a point to tell us that He has pre-pared a place for us, and the purpose of that place is for us to be together. The purpose of the cross was for us to be brought close together again. When He poured out His blood it did the amazing work of covering our rebellion against God, and made a way for us to come close because "now in Christ Jesus you who once were far away have been brought near through the blood of Christ!" If we are near, then we are free! We are free from fear, punishment, loneliness, and hopelessness! We are free to wor-ship!

This new freedom extends into the celebration of our relation-ship. The Bible underlines this truth: "Now the Lord is the

Spirit, and where the Spirit of the Lord is, there is freedom."

I will worship God.

I will worship God wild and loose.

Physical

Arts

Arms, legs, hands, feet, torso, head: all of these are composed of created matter.

All of these compose something far greater still.

The mind of man is a dream without me, and love for God is only a wish.

I am the worship of the body in motion.

A thought comes to life as I write or I speak. A passion stirs to express through my kissing and my holding. A love is embraced and I can feel the beauty of the moment. I have skin to feel, eyes to see, and ears to hear. I am the body, and I give to man what nothing else can give. I give the opportunity *to be* worship.

I kneel.

When I sense the presence of God I cannot help but bow. In all my glory I am but a glimpse of His reflection. I am so infinitely small in comparison. The weakness in my knees is a true and trembling response to the terrible love of God.

I reach.

I stretch my hands toward the heaven, expressing my attention to the Great One. My fingers signify the object of my affection that cannot be embraced on the earth. All attention is heavenward—the imagination's home for God. My face opens up to Him, full of expectation. Rain may fall to cool my tongue and clean my life. Words may come and touch my face with the truth. Like a child reaches for its father, I reach toward Him, and His mercy pours over my tender frame.

I dance.

My dance is not some mindless thing loosed on the earth to distract the eye from God. Quite the contrary, I reveal the eyes that are truly focused on God. I also reveal the heart of the worshiper. They must cooperate with me, or risk lying to their own hearts.

When the Lord touches my face I swoon and fall weak into His arms—how dare I stand proud and stiff? I sway with a sense of His own affection and rhythm to the beat of His heart. How could I refuse to enter the dance floor when the Lover of my soul has taken my hand? When the music of our love is at full crescendo I am drawn close to His face and forget my own presence as I fully yield to His. How could I spend time considering my reputation in view of the way He lost His own reputation for me? My dance may be graceful and quiet, but it, just as often, may be wild and unrestrained. I will be fully spent in dancing worship with Him, and I will celebrate His love in full view of the eyes of the world!

I am the worshiping body.

I am the kneeling, reaching, dancing body that must tell the truth:

Christ is worthy of my moving worship!

Price Of Romance

I heard wedding music.

In the exact moment that I realized who and what I was worshiping I heard wedding music.

The hand on my shoulder became the hand under my chin, lifting my head. I looked up into the most loving face I had ever seen. I was struck with the nearness, the inviting simplicity, of His look. He had not lost the explosive power when He came near, but it was contained in a different way. He looked like a man and a lion. His smile was also a roar. His hands were gentle as they drew me into the dance.

Round and round we went, past great fields of worshipers, dancers, and musicians playing the wildest of love songs. As we passed through each new meadow or planet or room the colors changed in response to our whirling, wonderful dance. This was not a melodrama where what is known is blown to a new proportion. This was a grand experience, totally new, and it was a thousand times larger and more truthful than any dream I had ever known. Every romance in the world reaches desperately to touch this one simple scene with the tip of its finger.

At the crescendo of the song we found ourselves standing on top of a very high mountain. The horizon swept wide and beautiful all around us. The air was thin and cold, but His hand on my shoulder warmed all of me.

He began to speak of His love for me without using words. Instead He showed me a picture. It was the picture of two beams of wood, one short, one long. They intersected each another. With one end the long beam heralded the sky and with the other it reached into the ground. The short beam pointed east to west. Suddenly the earth shook and the scene, now washed of color, was a heavily shadowed black and white. Here was my loving Rescuer, pinned to the wood by spikes through His wrists and feet. Pressed to the scene I could not escape the smell of hatred in the air, or the sound of gurgling in His throat as He labored to breathe. The blood that poured from His head and His body fell to the ground and ran toward all the nations of the earth. The ones He had been chasing had led Him here, the Pursuer had been pursued, and now the twisted justice of the unjust was piercing His body. Before I could even respond to the tragic image, a thunderclap…an explosion of power and light.

The scene was in color again. The cross still rose toward the heavens, defiantly now, from the bloodstained ground of the earth. And the Great Lover stood calmly in front of me, but high on the mountain. Like a scroll, a large banner opened up over the high place for all people of the earth to read:

Here is the One who is worthy,

He was slain,

and with His blood purchased people for God

from every tribe and language and people and nation.

A white robe descended from beyond the clouds. He dipped it in the blood that had pooled at the base of the cross, and when it was drenched in red He put it on. Then, taking His finger, in one great sweeping movement He drew a burning circle in the ground around the cross. I noticed that inside the circle the ground was perfectly flat, and though my description may not explain it, the circle was able to fully contain all the peoples of the earth—all who would come.

When He looked at me I said exactly what had been on my tongue to say since He had first lifted my head:

"Yes."

The Invitation

Enough Thoughts

Just to touch the face of God.

To find out who I really am.

It might be enough.

"Enough" is an incredible thought. When do we ever really have it? After we have eaten a large meal there is a sensation of "enough," but then a few hours later we are hungry again. Sometimes after the bonus paycheck we stare at our new account balance and feel a sense of "enough," but then just a few weeks later we are no longer satisfied with what we used to have. In the rush of accomplishment, for a moment there is "enough," but then comes the realization that all these things celebrated seem to fade. All the experiences of human life and the stuff of earth seem to turn with time from "enough" to "famine" at the end of every season.

But to connect to eternity...

To find a place in God...

Wouldn't this be *enough*?

The Followers of the Way seem to be proving it so. Maybe they are not proving it perfectly. Maybe they are not demonstrating every facet of it individually. As a community, however, they are revealing an amazing amount of *satisfaction*. The mystery that rock 'n' roll has never found, what philosophers have always searched for, and what religion has tried to pretend is found...

in the Circle of Worship around Jesus Christ.

Enough.

The people who have thoroughly touched and tested everything else often become the most satisfied Followers of the Way. There was once a woman who had tried a little bit of everything and ended up on the shattered end of the experiment. She was totally dissatisfied, but she tried very hard to look the part of the content woman while pushing the grocery cart of failure on the streets of her town. She met a man who pointed at the bucket of water she was drawing from the ancient well, and He said to her, "Everyone who drinks this water will be thirsty again, but whoever drinks the water I give him will never thirst. Indeed, the water I give him will become in him a spring of water welling up to eternal life." This common-looking man became the very uncommon Jesus who not only led this woman to admit her thirst for something lasting, but went on to provide her with exactly what He had promised—satisfaction. The water that He spoke of symbolized something deeper, something eternal and necessary. The new life that she received was wrapped up in their personal exchange—not some secondhand philosophy or enforcement of religious politics.

In the most apocalyptic passages of the Bible—the ones that make great movie sub-plots and "end time" discussions—we find the same, often overlooked, element—the promise of enough. As the future vision of the Book of Revelation was poured out on a Follower of the Way named John. He wrote, "Then the angel showed me the river of the water of life, as clear as crystal, flowing from the throne of God and of the Lamb down the middle of the great street of the city. On each side of the river stood the tree of life, bearing twelve crops of fruit, yielding its fruit every month. And the leaves of the tree are for the healing of the nations."

Amid all the images of war, and angels, and fire and locusts it is easy to miss the sweet ending of the apocalyptic vision.

The leaves of healing.

These leaves of healing, growing from the Tree of Life, are nurtured in the never-ending water that flows from the presence of God. It flows like a river from the Lamb of God, Christ Himself. The water symbolizes—the water actually is—something deeper. The Book of Revelation is less a prediction of the apocalyptic schedule and much more a reinforcement of the answer that Christ brings to all of human history—connection with the satisfying God.

The personal exchange that Christ offers is unlike any offer from any other spiritual salesman. He carries no product for selling, no teaching for secondhand adoption. He brings only Himself and offers only Himself, and in this exchange we can find everything we have been searching for.

We remember the claim that Christ made to the people gathered around Him, "Whoever believes in Me, as the Scripture has said, streams of living water will flow from within him." He was talking about the Spirit—the presence of God. I can hardly believe this is true. Nowhere else in all the world of religion and human effort is there found such a promise. If I were not aware of the Spirit of God living in me I could not believe. But I believe it is true! The God of creation, the pursuing God of love, has not offered us just answers or books or rituals or beliefs.

He has offered us much, much more.

A *connection* to the ultimate degree.

This is not some temporary arrangement whereby we can pull into the gas station of God and fill up with a little spiritual power and drive until the tank is empty again. This is a promise of an empowering, life-changing contact with God who actually *comes to live inside of us*. Unbelievable. We have heard spiritualists tells that we could talk to angels, and others say that we could become gods, and still others who tell us that through them or their disciplines we might gain temporary favor with the divine, but this is different. This is wild!

It is no wonder that Followers of the Way are so obsessed with worship. It is such an amazing thing to have the presence of God available at every moment!

Something must be done to express it!

We must express our sense of thanks, our sense of amazement, and our overwhelming joy!

These "streams of living water" that flow from inside of us are from God, and they fill us in order to flow out of us, and when the waters are released they pour out in wild, wonderful worship! They flow into our words as we speak and pray. They flow out onto the pages of our journals and into the poems of our experience. They flow onto the canvas of our expression and into the clay of our worship. They continue to flow and rush into every creative work, every wild dance, every loud song in an attempt to give some living expression to our adventure with God.

How can even the most well constructed dam hold back waters that never stop coming?

The flow is continuous.

It is powerful.

It is the water of life, and anyone who comes to Christ has full access.

Buzzz

Java Boy

I think the word is *epiphany*—a nice, poetic word. Everything seemed to be coming together. I was getting it. I was sitting in a room with a bunch of people who seemed to be "getting it" as well.

The chant had given way to a fury of drumming and dancing and celebration. People in varying moods of dress were pounding on African drums, Latin drums, and Asian drums. Dancers were whirling around the front and throwing themselves at God in open-arm gestures all over the room. I had never seen such public abandonment to the belief that God was that *real*...that *present*.

I speak about it now with more understanding than I had that night, but I was aware of the simple truth of it even then. It was all about giving thanks and praise and love to God, and it was all wrapped up in Jesus.

These people were in love with Jesus.

I knew parts of the Bible, but never in my life would I have woven what I thought I knew into the scene that was played out in front of me. I had no idea that Jesus represented so much of God's love for us, or that people could spend so much of themselves trying to express their gratitude for Him.

I had also never seen the cross the way I saw it that first night at the worship gathering. Songs filled my mind with images of Christ and why He died on the cross. Paintings depicted His outstretched hands and the crown and banner over His head. There was poetry and pottery and prayers that all spoke about a vision of the cross I had never seen before. My mind was spinning with these pictures and the words of one of the poets:

The cross neither jewelry, nor icon, nor charm,

The cross held a lover who died in my arms

Under the weight of the hammer I held

The space between heaven and everything

Spanned

And the lost art of living was found again

When the cross became loving and Christ became friend.

There was Chris, on her knees near the stage with her arm around someone who was weeping. The drum circle had evolved into a steady rhythm. It sounded like a beating heart. And deep down in the private place of my heart I could feel the unmistakable word forming on the mouth of my soul:

"Yes."

I knew it was an answer to me from the God I had been searching for.

"Yes."

I knew it was my answer to Him as I considered His call to me from the cross.

"Yes."

I had a strange feeling that soon I would be kneeling near the stage. I hoped that someone like Chris would put a hand on my shoulder and pray for me.

Enter The Worship Circle

No one can hand it to us.

But the Worship Circle might be the place where we find what we have been looking for. Jesus Christ just might be revealing the God we have been dreaming about. The Followers of the Way just might be holding the keys to unlock our supernatural adventure into eternity.

Where will we begin?

The Bible is not a scientific book. It does not seek to put human experience in a test tube and break down the elements into clean categories. The Bible is a book of mystical experience. Where there is history, there is divine intervention. Where there is poetry, there is supernatural inspiration. Where there is a prophet, there is a claim to carry a message from beyond. Where there is any action or relationship in the Bible, there is always a transcendent issue.

The Bible does not point to itself, it points to Christ. It might be one of the best places to start our journey.

What if divine communication did not stop when the writers of the Bible put down their pens? What if God is still actively expressing His heart to us today? Maybe the busy sounds of television, music, and buzzing modems are masking His voice—or maybe they contain it. If He is still speaking then, with no experience in things spiritual and with no understanding of the writing in the Bible, we are free to listen for God. If He loves us, then He can meet us and speak to us where we are. Reaching out like a child toward the face of God may be a good way to continue.

Christianity is a bizarre and conflicted collection of people and traditions in our modern world. We could visit a dozen churches and not find one where we felt the presence of God or any hope of connecting to Him.

But there is always visit number thirteen.

There *are* Followers of the Way who still meet in Christian churches. Some of these churches meet in old buildings, some in shopping mall spaces, and some in people's homes. The Followers sometimes meet in very untraditional places like coffeehouses, art galleries, or concert halls. Often there are Followers of the Way and Followers of Dead Tradition meeting in the same room, and sometimes it is difficult to know who is who. What should we do? I believe it would be worth the effort to get into the mix. It would be worth it to find some fellow seekers—some fellow worshipers. Joining a group of Followers for worship and Bible study could be worth all the effort, and all the careful searching, if the beginning of a relationship with God can be nurtured.

Any way we choose to begin we still have to make the choice.

And no one can hand it to us.

We could choose to live our life here on earth, or we could choose to go beyond it. Do we believe that what we see is all there is? Or is something gnawing at the back of our minds telling us there is something more? We can curl up and die with what we know, or we can dive out of the high-rise dream and fall headlong into a deeper reality.

The deeper reality is God.

The new activity is worship.

Worship gatherings are not perfect; the Followers of the Way are not perfect either, but the God they adore is. God will have His way with His broken followers, and He could have His wonderful, healing way with us if would make the choice to follow Him as well.

We don't have to take a stranger's word for it. We can find out for ourselves.

It is time to make a move. It is time to put forth some effort on behalf of the God who has pursued through all these years of our indifference.

It is time to enter the Worship Circle. The following Path of Seven can be enjoyed in a public group or in a private place:

1. While others are worshiping in music and song set up a canvas or spread out your drawing paper. Ask the Lord to speak to your heart. Whatever you "see" or "hear" put onto the surface with your medium of choice. Move with the music what you sense from God. Reflect back to God what you think He is saying to you. Try to give others a chance to watch the process.

2. Pull out a notebook and a pen. During a worship event take the time to write down colorful description of all that you see around you. Freely examine the worship environment and look for the movement of the Spirit of God. When a picture of His beauty comes clear, write down your love in a poem. Write down your adoration in prose. Let it flow. Don't hold back. There are no words too grand for God!

3. On your instrument or with instrumental music playing sing a new song to God. Make it a love song. You may first sing a passage of the Bible as you look at the written page—maybe from the Psalms—but then you must sing your own love

words to God. Throw your head back and let Him hear it. Sing of His love! Call for His help! Sing to Him whatever is on your heart!

4. Find some modeling clay. Whether professional or novice you can offer up to God the work of your hands. Ask God to speak to your heart before you begin to worship, and then press into being whatever He shows you. Breathe your prayers as you go, and at the end of the worship time share your heart with others about what God was speaking to you.

5. Bring a hand drum or shaker or some simple rhythm instrument to a worship event. As worship begins listen for the sound of heaven. Ask the Holy Spirit to help you release that sound into the worship. Listen carefully to other worshipers and ebb and flow with them. Enjoy the family collaboration. Pray for others as you play and speak simple phrases of love into every rhythmic phrase.

6. Stand near the edge of the worship event and take in all the movement, all the singing, and all the visuals with your eyes open. After a few moments close your eyes and lift your face toward God. Lift your hands toward Him too. Stretch yourself out and abandon yourself to Him. He is trustworthy! Move as He leads you!

7. In the energy of good worship music find an open place to stand. Sing the songs, and make your love known to God. Ask God to come and show you how to dance. Ask Him to come and dance with you. Now let it go, and have fun! Quit thinking! Enjoy Him! Enjoy the music! Enjoy giving yourself totally to God, and move your body to show your love.

Wine For A Wedding

In this final scene of the vision I cannot begin to tell of all the things that were revealed. For me it was both the beginning and the end.

The long table was set with food and decoration more lavish than any I had ever seen. One end stopped right before the great white throne of God, but I could not see the other end of it as it stretched to a fine point in the distance. Names of the worshipers were carved into the heads of the chairs. Their first names were unique but their surnames were all the same—the secret name of God.

The multitudes who sang and played instruments numbered in the tens of thousands, and the dancing and laughing and kissing and twirling was wild and free. In the center of it all, to my amazement, was the Pursuing God Himself, caught up in the most wonderful dance I had ever witnessed. It was both absurd and beautiful. It did not stir embarrassment, however, because there was no more shame. The entire crowd loved it. I loved it. And in a moment we were all inspired to take to the floor and join in the dancing.

Men, women, and children of every race, nation, and history celebrated this amazing feast. The glory that came with them—the colors, the culture, the legends—were draped over the great white throne, and occasionally the Lord would take one of the tapestries and run with it streaming in flowing waves behind Him.

Our wineglasses full, we praised and thanked and honored our Pursuing God for what seemed like a thousand years.

When the time had come, He stood, holding a glass, and holding His arms out to us all. As He drew in His breath to speak a hush blanketed the whole assembly. His eyes filled with love and brimmed with tears as he spoke.

"My dear, lovely bride. Today the dreams of my heart are all woven together in you. The 'yes' you have spoken to Me has made your mouth more beautiful than it was the day I whispered the first kiss of life into it. Now you are old enough for love, and this day I will take you as my wife!"

Cheers, screaming, crying, and a thunderous wave of applause filled the great ballroom. The old world and all its memories were fading away. All things were becoming new. It was both a beginning and an end.

"My dear beautiful bride." He paused to consider us with His loving eyes and then He spoke again with great assurance, "The words I spoke concerning the cup of intimacy in ancient times is fulfilled today in your presence. Today is the day—the cornerstone of eternity—when you will no longer call Me your Master, but from now on you will call Me your Husband. Let's drink in celebration of My new name as well as yours since, from this day on I will always call you My Wife!"

As the wineglasses lifted and the celebrants cheered, I fell faint onto the floor.

Music drifted into a distant corner of my mind.

I could feel my back pressed firmly into the floor.

I could hear my name and feel someone touching my shoulder.

"Wake up, we have to go," urged the familiar voice, and suddenly I sat up in the room where we met for worship. My skirt was awkwardly wound around my legs. The band was breaking down their instruments and the canvases and pottery wheel were being moved back to the storage room. Most had already filtered out of the room into the cool Colorado air, making their way home or out somewhere for food. I turned to my friend while still struggling to regain my senses and said: "There is no way you are going to believe what I saw tonight."

"Really. Well, you have been on the floor for hours."

I rubbed my forehead. My head hurt a little.

"Have you met Java Boy yet?" he continued. "You know, Mr. Coffee-Is-Life? The guy is fixated on Chris's art so we're going over to the café."

Fumbling around for my things I was only half listening to him, I grabbed my jacket and we headed out the door. As the cool air met my face I realized that the vision was not going to stay behind in the safety of the warm gathering room. My mind was swimming with the images and words I had experienced.

I did not want to forget.

I thought I could still hear the wedding music, faint underneath our footsteps, as the cold air turned our walk into a run.

The Greatful Author

I have come to realize that all of my creative effort reflects the places, adventures, and people of my life. Very little is birthed from a "clean slate." In some way, everything that has touched me goes on to touch what I think, what I do, and what I imagine. From this stream of experience I would like to hold up a few people that deserve specific recognition for contributing to the "imagining" in this book.

Thanks first to my lovely wife whose insights and loving nature help my creativity develop a crisp, clear focus.

Thanks to our editing team, scattered across the country, for helping this book find a comfortable fit in the hands of many more people.

Thanks to Boyd Dupree for his genius in creating images that transcend the tools of his trade.

Thanks to the people at Relevant Media Group whose vision for creating this kind of work may change the world as we know it. Rather than coloring outside the lines of the Christian culture, they have simply chosen to believe there are no lines.

Thanks to GrassRoots Music and the unapologetic approach they have taken to providing music for people who enjoy spiritual dialogue, but choke on religion.

Thanks to Ravi Zacharias and the courage he has shown in providing stiff challenge to those who might pause and consider eternity. His book, Can Man Live Without God?, offers up a brilliant collection of thoughts for the modern person in search of God. It was from this book that I first encountered the inspiring idea of God being the "Ultimate Novelty."

For more insights into the world of worship and of the creative work around these themes visit *www.EnterTheWorshipCircle.com*.

Notes

Notes

Notes

Notes

Notes

You've read the book.
Now experience the music.
ENTER THE WORSHIP CIRCLE:
Second Circle
Enter the Worship Circle
SECOND CIRCLE
the new album
In stores nationwide or online at
www.grassrootsmusic.com
Distributed by Grassroots Music Distribution
www.grassroots.mu / 800-578-3278

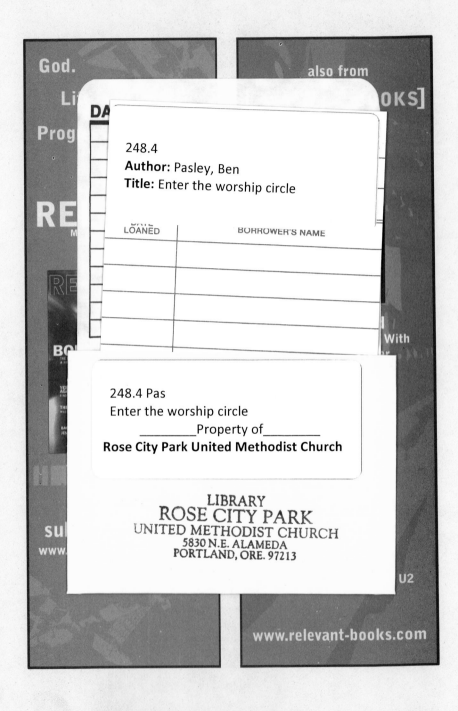

www.relevant-books.com